Jesus of Nazareth

by William W. Lace

LUCENT BOOKS
An imprint of Thomson Gale, a part of The Thomson Corporation

Detroit • New York • San Francisco • San Diego • New Haven, Conn. • Waterville, Maine • London • Munich

© 2006 Thomson Gale, a part of The Thomson Corporation.

Thomson and Star Logo are trademarks and Gale and Lucent Books are registered trademarks used herein under license.

For more information, contact
Lucent Books
27500 Drake Rd.
Farmington Hills, MI 48331-3535
Or you can visit our Internet site at http://www.gale.com

ALL RIGHTS RESERVED.
No part of this work covered by the copyright hereon may be reproduced or used in any form or by any means—graphic, electronic, or mechanical, including photocopying, recording, taping, Web distribution, or information storage retrieval systems—without the written permission of the publisher.

Every effort has been made to trace the owners of copyrighted material.

LIBRARY OF CONGRESS CATALOGING-IN-PUBLICATION DATA

Lace, William W.
  Jesus of Nazareth / by William W. Lace.
    p. cm. — (The importance of)
  Includes bibliographical references and index.
  Contents: Bethlehem—Nazareth—The Jordan—Galilee—Jerusalem—Golgotha—Aftermath. ISBN 1-59018-640-0 (hardcover : alk. paper)
  1. Jesus Christ—Biography. I. Title. II. Series.
BT301.3.L33 2005
232.9'01—dc22
                                                        2004030211

Printed in the United States of America

Contents

Foreword — 5
Important Dates in the Time of Jesus of Nazareth — 6
Introduction
    So Much from So Little — 8
Chapter 1
    Bethlehem — 13
Chapter 2
    Nazareth — 28
Chapter 3
    The Jordan — 40
Chapter 4
    Galilee — 53
Chapter 5
    Jerusalem — 70
Chapter 6
    Golgotha — 81
Epilogue
    Aftermath — 93

Notes — 98
For Further Reading — 101
Works Consulted — 102
Index — 105
Picture Credits — 111
About the Author — 112

Foreword

The Importance Of biography series deals with individuals who have made a unique contribution to history. The editors of the series have deliberately chosen to cast a wide net and include people from all fields of endeavor. Individuals from politics, music, art, literature, philosophy, science, sports, and religion are all represented. In addition, the editors did not restrict the series to individuals whose accomplishments have helped change the course of history. Of necessity, this criterion would have eliminated many whose contribution was great, though limited. Charles Darwin, for example, was responsible for radically altering the scientific view of the natural history of the world. His achievements continue to impact the study of science today. Others, such as Chief Joseph of the Nez Percé, played a pivotal role in the history of their own people. While Joseph's influence does not extend much beyond the Nez Percé, his nonviolent resistance to white expansion and his continuing role in protecting his tribe and his homeland remain an inspiration to all.

These biographies are more than factual chronicles. Each volume attempts to emphasize an individual's contributions both in his or her own time and for posterity. For example, the voyages of Christopher Columbus opened the way to European colonization of the New World. Unquestionably, his encounter with the New World brought monumental changes to both Europe and the Americas in his day. Today, however, the broader impact of Columbus's voyages is being critically scrutinized. Christopher Columbus, as well as every biography in The Importance Of series, includes and evaluates the most recent scholarship available on each subject.

Each author includes a wide variety of primary and secondary source quotations to document and substantiate his or her work. All quotes are footnoted to show readers exactly how and where biographers derive their information, as well as provide stepping stones to further research. These quotations enliven the text by giving readers eyewitness views of the life and times of each individual covered in The Importance Of series.

Finally, each volume is enhanced by photographs, bibliographies, chronologies, and comprehensive indexes. For both the casual reader and the student engaged in research, The Importance Of biographies will be a fascinating adventure into the lives of people who have helped shape humanity's past and present, and who will continue to shape its future.

Important Dates in the Time of Jesus of Nazareth

4 B.C. King Herod ("the Great") dies.

A.D. 14 Augustus Caesar, emperor of Rome, dies.

A.D. 1 Chiefdoms begin to form in South America's Amazon basin.

10 B.C.   A.D. 1   10 A.D.   20 A.D.

c. 7 B.C. Jesus is born in Bethlehem.

c. A.D. 5 Jesus debates with scholars in the temple at Jerusalem.

A.D. 18 Joseph Caiaphas becomes high priest in Jerusalem.

A.D. 26 Pontius Pilate becomes governor of Judea.

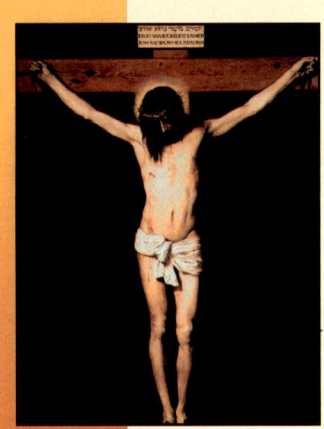

c. A.D. 30
Jesus is tried and crucified in Jerusalem.

A.D. 58
Buddhism is introduced in China.

A.D. 43
Roman Emperor Claudius Augustus invades Britain.

A.D. 64
St. Peter and St. Paul are executed in Rome.

30 A.D.   40 A.D.   50 A.D.   60 A.D.   A.D. 70

A.D. 36
Joseph Caiaphas and Pontius Pilate are removed from office.

A.D. 50
The Pyramid of the Sun is built in Mexico.

A.D. 70
Roman legions destroy the temple in Jerusalem.

c. A.D. 27
Jesus begins his ministry.

Introduction

So Much from So Little

Jesus of Nazareth, according to the Book of Matthew, told his disciples (28:20), "And lo, I am with you always."[1] Indeed, his image and impact are almost inescapable in parts of the world where Christianity is dominant.

The cross, symbol of his death and—his followers believe—his ultimate victory over death, sits atop church steeples in every town and city. Whether made of simple wood or precious metals, it hangs on chains around countless necks, sometimes as much a statement of fashion as of faith.

The supposed likenesses of this humble, Jewish carpenter adorn billboards, bumper stickers, and T-shirts. His name is used daily in expressions, not only of reverence, but also of amazement or even anger.

Christianity is the most prevalent religion on earth, espoused by one of every three people. And even in areas of the world that are not Christian, Jesus's name and teachings have been carried by generations of missionaries.

Given his pervasive presence, Jesus of Nazareth is the most important person in human history. And yet, for all the impact made by this single life, very few details of it are known. In fact, not a single fact regarding Jesus is historically verifiable.

The Gospels

There are no firsthand accounts of Jesus's life. Most of what has come down through the millennia is contained in the first four books of the New Testament, known as the Gospels, attributed to Matthew, Mark, Luke, and John. Tradition holds that two of the authors—Matthew and John—were among Jesus's disciples, but most scholars think that the Gospels were written forty to seventy years after his death.

The lack of firsthand accounts is not surprising. After his execution by the

Romans in about A.D. 30 and—Christians believe—his resurrection, Jesus told his disciples that he would return. His earliest followers likely thought this "second coming" would be in a matter of weeks—a few months at the most. But as the years passed and those who had known Jesus died, Christians probably saw the need to collect what people remembered, or had been told, that he had said or done.

Also, the authors of the Gospel wrote about Jesus from specific points of view, to convey different concepts to different audiences at different times. Consequently, it is very difficult to know which parts are biography and which are allegory, never designed to be taken as fact. This is especially true since the Gospels frequently disagree, contradicting themselves in important ways.

Moreover, these four Gospels are by no means the only ones. The author of Luke, in his opening sentence (1:1), notes that "many have undertaken to compile a narrative of the things which have been accomplished among us." Indeed, there

This twelfth-century Italian painting depicts Jesus of Nazareth after he was crucified and rose from the dead.

are numerous Gospels claiming to be accounts of Jesus's life and teaching written by eyewitnesses such as Peter, Mary Magdalene, Thomas, and many others.

Why, then, does every child in Sunday school know of Matthew, Mark, Luke, and John while the others have been consigned to history's dark corners? The answer lies almost seventeen hundred years in the past.

Before the invention of the printing press in the fifteenth century, Bibles were copied by hand and lavishly illustrated. Pictured is a page from a twelfth-century Bible.

Constantine's Book

The Roman emperor Constantine, who raised Christianity from persecution to prominence in the early 300s, commissioned fifty copies of a book to contain the religion's most sacred texts. Before such a book could be compiled, church leaders had to decide exactly what should be included and, almost as important, excluded.

Throughout its early history, Christianity was torn by disagreements over who Jesus was and what he taught. Perhaps the most bitter controversy concerned Jesus's basic nature. Had he been both human and divine or entirely divine?

One group of Christians, very influential at the time Constantine's book was being compiled, was the Gnostics, so-called because they believed that salvation came from secret knowledge (*gnosis* in Greek) revealed by God. Their view that Jesus was wholly divine did not prevail against those who argued for his dual nature, and their writings, which emphasized only the divine nature, were eliminated. Such works and others not included in the Bible are sometimes called apocryphal, from a Greek word meaning "hidden [*apokruphos*]."

The accepted writings became part of what is known as the canon, from the Greek word for a measuring stick (*kanon*), since they met the requirements of the majority opinion. Both the canonical and noncanonical Gospels, however, probably came from the same or similar sources—sayings attributed to Jesus and stories about his life and deeds that had been handed down through the generations, filtered through various theological views.

The "Q" Source

Mark is thought to be the oldest of the canonical Gospels, but scholars think that the author drew on an older source, now lost, called proto-Mark. Similarly, Matthew and Luke, while they use some of Mark's material, contain much more, leading to speculation that they used a common document scholars call "Q," from the German word for "source" (*quelle*).

No one can be sure if the Gospels—canonical and noncanonical—have survived in their original forms. Some experts think that Matthew, Mark, Luke, and John underwent considerable editing, with material added or deleted according to the beliefs of the time. Furthermore, some of the noncanonical Gospels are little more than fragments, such as those found in Egypt in 1945.

References to Jesus by non-Christians during his life are nonexistent, and those

The "Q" Source

No one is sure exactly who wrote the four Gospels. Likewise, no one can be certain where the authors, whoever they were, obtained their information.

Three Gospels—Matthew, Mark, and Luke—are called the synoptic Gospels because they generally share the same content and style. Mark is considered to have been the first Gospel written, and the authors of Luke and Matthew seem to have relied on Mark for information. Much material in Luke and Matthew, however, is not found in Mark.

Biblical scholars have speculated that Luke and Matthew must have used an earlier Gospel, now lost, that was unavailable to Mark. They named this lost work "Q," for the German word *quelle*, or "source."

"Q" is thought to be the source for many of Jesus's sayings, including the Lord's Prayer, and some of the stories found nowhere else, such as the details of the temptation in the wilderness. It was probably written before the conquest of Jerusalem by the Romans in A.D. 70, which would place it earlier than Mark.

in the years after his death—except for those proven to be forgeries, such as supposed letters from Pontius Pilate, the Roman governor at the time—concern the early Christians, not Jesus. The exception is by Flavius Josephus, a Jewish historian writing about A.D. 90. Even this source is highly suspect since Josephus calls Jesus "the Christ"[2] (or savior), something a Jew would never do. Since it was not until the 300s that any record is found of Josephus having mentioned Jesus, many scholars think it was added by Christian scribes.

Of such bits and pieces is the life of Jesus of Nazareth to be reconstructed. Most of the people who wrote about him were not attempting to write a biography in the modern sense. They were describing Christ the god, not Jesus the man.

Some scholars, indeed, question whether Jesus ever existed at all. Such a view seems extreme. He was very likely a real person—a Jew in first-century Palestine who gathered a band of followers, led the life of a wandering preacher, and was finally executed as a perceived danger to the established order. This much seems likely, though by no means certain. What is certain, however, is that his life, which went largely unnoticed at the time, touched the lives of others, some of whom went on to establish one of the world's great religions in his name.

Chapter 1

Bethlehem

St. Paul, the primary architect of Christianity, wrote to the church he established in Corinth (II Corinthians 5:16) that "even though we once regarded [Jesus] Christ from a human point of view, we regard him thus no longer." This is precisely the problem in trying to piece together the life of Jesus from the Gospels. The authors were intent on telling the story of the Christ of faith, not the Jesus of history.

Nowhere is this more evident than in the accounts of his birth. As Biblical scholar Hendrikus Boers writes, "The legends of his birth and infancy do not provide historical data about Jesus but rather express who he was. . . . The legends, including the stories of divine intervention in connection with his birth, are tools used by New Testament Christians to express their perception of Jesus."[3]

The Gospel authors believed Jesus to have been divine, and in the ancient world, divinity was frequently connected with a miraculous birth. It was believed that extraordinary beings must have extraordinary origins. The Greek hero Hercules was supposedly the son of the god Jove. Emperor Yu of China was said to have been conceived when his mother was struck by a star. The Egyptian pharaohs were considered gods born in human form who returned to being purely gods after death.

While many Christians believe that Jesus's birth took place exactly as described in the Gospels, most theologians think that the Nativity stories were the writers' versions of what they believed must have occurred. This is not to say that the authors were liars or charlatans, weaving fantasies in order to bolster their individual viewpoints. Their ardent belief in Jesus's divinity convinced them that his birth was a miracle. And since Jesus was a Jew believed by his followers to be the Messiah, or savior, predicted in Judaism,

Shepherds worship the newborn Jesus in this Italian painting. Although many works of art show the baby Jesus in a stable, the Bible does not mention one.

they likely reconstructed the story by seizing on bits of Old Testament prophecy and scraps of oral tradition, connecting these dots and coloring the spaces in between. As theologian John Dominic Crossan writes, "The transcendental importance of the adult Jesus" made it necessary for early writers to "retroject that importance onto the conception and birth itself."[4]

Writing from Belief

It should be no surprise, then, that the Gospel accounts of Jesus's birth vary, in some cases dramatically. Different authors emphasized different prophecies. Sometimes the same prophecy was worked into the narratives in different ways. Then, too, the authors' individual beliefs came into play. It would be natural, for instance, to speculate that Jesus's mother said a prayer of gratitude, but the wording of that prayer might reflect the author's theological bias.

While many of the events connected with the Nativity of Jesus are uncertain, the political climate is not. First-century Palestine was a cauldron of discontent as the Jews found themselves almost aliens in their own land. Politically, the Romans dominated Palestine and, indeed, most of the known world. Judea, the part of Palestine in which Jesus was born, was ruled by King Herod, nominally a Jew but actually of Arab descent and a close ally of Rome. The people were heavily taxed, both by Rome and by Herod.

Herod

One of the great villains of history, Herod "the Great," was, according to the Gospels, king of Judea at the time of Jesus's birth. In fact, however, Herod was not even a Jew, ethnically speaking, although he practiced Judaism.

When the Roman general Pompey invaded Palestine in 63 B.C., Antipater, a wealthy Arab ruler in the area of Edom, aided him. The family became close allies of Rome, and Antipater and his son Herod were on intimate terms with such people as Julius Caesar, Mark Anthony, and Augustus Caesar. Antipater was made governor of Judea in 47 B.C., and Herod succeeded him on his assassination four years later.

The Roman senate made Herod king of Judea in 40 B.C., and he held onto the title ruthlessly for thirty-six years. His reign was marked by grandiose building projects, including the Temple in Jerusalem.

Herod was deeply suspicious and murdered anyone he thought a threat to him, including his wife and two of his sons. He is best known for supposedly ordering all male children in Bethlehem two years old and under to be killed, having heard that a new king—Jesus—had been born there.

After learning that a new king had been born in Bethlehem, King Herod, pictured in this mosaic, ordered the slaughter of all infant boys there.

Bethlehem 15

Palestine's culture, as well, was increasingly alien to the Jews. Ever since the area had been conquered by Alexander the Great more than three hundred years earlier, the Hellenistic, or Greek, culture had grown more prevalent. New cities were built in the Greco-Roman style, complete with temples to gods considered by the Jews a blasphemous affront to the God they believed to exist to the exclusion of all others. Some upper-class Jews, however, gravitated toward Hellenistic culture, speaking Greek and drifting away from traditional Judaism.

Awaiting Deliverance

Thus, their livelihoods threatened by heavy taxation and their culture and religion steadily undermined, the great body of conservative Jews looked for deliverance. The deliverer, many thought, would be the promised Messiah who would reestablish the kingdom made powerful by the hero David about 970 B.C. Jesus of Nazareth, his followers believed, was this savior, miraculously sent to earth by God.

So which parts of the Gospel accounts of Jesus's birth are historically verifiable? None, with the exception of some historical characters, such as Herod and the Roman emperor Augustus, who are known to have lived. However, saying that the Nativity story may not have occurred entirely as set down is not to say that none of it took place. The similarities of the Gospels make it likely that Jesus was born a Jew, that he was born in the Judean town of Bethlehem, that his mother was a young woman named Miryam (Mary in English), and that his father—earthly father, at least—was named Yusuf (Joseph). Everything beyond this—all the treasured parts of the Christmas story—are matters of faith or, as English writer Malcolm Muggeridge put it, "the domain of the imagination, not the intellect."[5]

The New Testament Gospels say almost nothing about the backgrounds of Mary and Joseph except to trace Joseph's ancestry to David, since it had been prophesied that the Messiah would be of the house of David. Both Matthew and Luke contain such genealogies, and they serve as good examples of how various authors suited the text to their own purpose. Matthew wrote from a distinctly Jewish point of view, and his lineage goes back to Abraham, father of the Jewish people. Luke, however, is thought by many scholars to have been a Greek and seems to intend his Gospel for a gentile, or non-Jewish, audience. He takes the genealogy further, all the way back to Adam, the first man according to the Book of Genesis in the Old Testament, thus getting across his theme that Jesus was intended as savior of all people, not just the Jews.

Mary's Background

While little concerning Mary and Joseph is to be found in the Bible, the noncanonical Gospels contain much more about Jesus's parents, especially Mary. Her birthplace has been put variously at Nazareth,

This portrayal of Mary, mother of Jesus, was done by the Renaissance master Raphael. The Bible says very little about her background.

Sepphoris, Bethlehem, and Jerusalem. According to the Gospel of James, Mary's father was named Joachim and her mother Anna. Her birth was said to be something of a miracle in itself, since her parents were very elderly and had almost given up hope of having children. Anna, however, prayed so fervently that an angel appeared and told her she would bear a child. Overjoyed, Anna promised to dedicate the child, male or female, to God.

The story of Mary's birth appears to be a clear parallel to the similar Old Testament story of Isaac being born to Abraham and Sarah in their old age. In both cases, God has taken a direct part in a child's conception.

Jewish law required that all firstborn males be presented in the Temple in Jerusalem and dedicated to God, but the same ritual could be done with other highly favored children, including—very rarely—daughters. According to the Gnostic tradition, Mary was presented to the Temple, holiest place in Judaism and headquarters of the chief priests, when she was three years old. She is said to have climbed the steep stairs, taken a vow of perpetual virginity, and been granted certain unnamed supernatural powers.

Mary supposedly remained in the Temple to be raised and educated by the priests, something extremely unlikely in view of the subordinate roles of women in the Judaism of the time. When she was twelve years old and about to reach puberty, she could no longer stay in the Temple and "perchance . . . defile the sanctuary of the Lord."[6] The high priest prayed and was told by God to select a husband for her from among the men of the house of David. Joseph was chosen, supposedly when his rod, or walking stick, sprouted a dove—traditionally the sign of God's spirit—that settled on his head. Mary and Joseph were promptly betrothed.

Mary's Divinity

These Gnostic Gospel accounts of Mary, while appealing, have no parallels in the Bible and are not recognized by the Christian church. The reason is not that they are any more or less historically verifiable than the New Testament version. Rather, the problem with them, at least from the standpoint of those who compiled the canon, was they make Mary seem divine in her own right, thus diminishing the human aspect of her son, Jesus. Those who held that Jesus was entirely divine needed Mary to be divine, as well. The orthodox view that prevailed in the end was that Mary was an ordinary, though very devout, young woman.

She was, indeed—both Matthew and Luke write—betrothed to Joseph. Betrothal, however, had a different meaning than it does today. Rather than an informal engagement to be married, it was a binding contract. The woman became, in effect, the man's property, although the actual marriage would not take place for about a year. In some areas of Palestine, the man and women could engage in sexual intercourse, although they lived apart. If the man died during the betrothal period, the woman would be considered his widow.

It was evidently during this betrothal period that Joseph and Mary are said to have been told that Mary was to bear a son who would be named Jesus (Yeshua in Hebrew). In Luke's Gospel an angel appeared to Mary, while in Matthew's version an angel appeared to Joseph. The angels delivered the same message—that Mary would give birth to a son conceived by the Holy Spirit. This is a fulfillment of the prophecy of Isaiah (7:14): "Therefore the Lord Himself will give you a sign: Behold, a virgin will be with child and bear a son, and she will call His name Immanuel [Hebrew for 'God with us']."

The Virgin Birth

One of the basic traditions of Christianity is that Jesus's birth was extraordinary in that his mother, Mary, was a virgin. Instead of having an earthly father, the Gospels of Matthew and Luke say, Mary conceived by the power of God—that is, the Holy Spirit. In the discussion of Jesus's birth in his Life of Jesus, *Professor Barry Smith writes that the concept of a virgin birth is not found in Judaism:*

One does not find the idea that the Messiah would be born of a virgin through the action of the Holy Spirit, and by virtue of this action be the son of God, in the surviving second-Temple Jewish literature. The idea of the Messiah's virginal origin is discontinuous with Jewish messianic expectation; it appears to be unique to the New Testament. . . . Most scholars account for its emergence as resulting from the influence of the Hellenistic idea of the "divine man" . . . An early christological reflection. The divine man is a man with divinely-given supernatural abilities.

Although the Bible states that Mary was a virgin, some scholars think the story was created to emphasize Jesus's divinity.

Mary greeted the angel's announcement with amazement and asked how such a thing could happen since she was a virgin. The angel, named by Luke as Gabriel, answered (1:35) that the "Holy Spirit will come upon you, and the power of the Most High will overshadow you."

The Translation Issue

The virgin birth is perhaps the most controversial aspect of the story of Jesus. For many Christians, it is absolutely essential, demonstrating that Jesus was both human and divine. Others point to the ancient Greek translation of the Old Testament, from which Matthew and Luke probably worked, and how it mistranslated the Hebrew word *almah*, meaning "young woman," as "virgin." They say that it is Jesus's subsequent life, not his birth, that is important.

Stories of virgins conceiving and giving birth to extraordinary children, however, were common in the ancient world. The Hindu god Krishna, the Aztec gods Quexalcote and Citlatonac, the Persian prophet Zoroaster, and many others were said to have been born of virgin mothers. There was no such tradition, however, in Judaism, which causes some scholars to think that the story may have been told in order to appeal to non-Jews.

Nowhere are the Gospel contradictions more pronounced than in the stories of Jesus's birth. The earliest Gospel, Mark, does not mention it at all. Neither do the many epistles, or letters, of Paul, written even earlier. It is not until Matthew and Luke, both thought to have been written sometime after A.D. 70, that the subject is addressed. These omissions lead some critics to dismiss the entire story. As historian J.R. Porter writes,

> One of the strongest arguments against the authenticity of the virgin birth is that apart from Matthew and Luke the new Testament never refers to it—in contrast to the central position of the Resurrection. Of course, this is an argument from silence and it may be that the virgin birth began as a private tradition within Jesus' own family, and only became more widely known with the increasing desire to learn more of Jesus' early life.[7]

After the angel departed, Luke writes, Mary went to the home of her cousin, Elizabeth, who was pregnant with a son who would become John the Baptist, a significant figure in Jesus's life. Like Mary's parents, Elizabeth and her husband, Zechariah, had been childless in their old age but their prayers for a child had been answered by God in the form of an angel, yet another parallel with the Old Testament story of Isaac. The relationship of Jesus to John is foreshadowed in Luke when, on hearing Mary's voice, the baby in Elizabeth's womb "leaped for joy" (1:44).

Zechariah's Prediction

Later, when John was born, his father foresaw great things for him. His prediction that John "will go before the Lord to prepare his ways" (Luke 1:76) is highly significant since it places John in a subordinate role to Jesus. Some experts think it was made a part of the story because, even after the deaths of both John and Jesus, some people believed John, not Jesus, to be the Messiah.

Where all these events took place depends on which Gospel one reads. Matthew says nothing about Joseph and Mary living in Nazareth, only that Jesus was born in Bethlehem. Luke places Mary specifically in Nazareth, a small village in the northern Palestinian area of Galilee, when she was visited by Gabriel. He goes on to say, however, that Elizabeth's house was in Judea, meaning that Mary would have to have undertaken a journey of several days, presumably alone. If Mary already lived in Bethlehem, however, she probably could have gone to and returned from her cousin's house in a single day.

Jesus's entire connection with Nazareth, in fact, is very obscure. Matthew cites a prophecy—"He shall be called a Nazarene" (2:23)—in placing Jesus there after his birth. No such prophecy has ever been discovered in Jewish literature. In fact, there is no mention of Nazareth in any listing of Palestinian towns before about

Mary reveals her pregnancy to her cousin, Elizabeth, in this fifteenth-century Italian painting. Elizabeth would also bear a son, who would become John the Baptist.

A.D. 300, and some scholars have speculated that the tradition of Jesus living there is a result of a mistranslation of the Hebrew word *notsri*, which can mean "watcher" or "keeper" and is one way the earliest Christians referred to themselves.

The oldest parts of present-day Nazareth, however, do date from Jesus's time, so the tradition that he lived there may well be true.

Bethlehem

On the other hand, Bethlehem, while perhaps not a large city, was highly significant in Jewish history. It is mentioned in Egyptian records as old as 1400 B.C. It was the burial place of Rachel, favorite wife of Abraham's grandson Jacob, and, more important for Jesus's history, the birthplace of the shepherd boy who later became King David. As opposed to Nazareth, the prophecy concerning Bethlehem is clear (Micah 5:2): "But you, O Bethlehem Ephrathah, who are little to be among the clans of Judah, from you shall come forth for me one who is to be ruler in Israel, whose origin is from of old, from ancient days."

The tradition, then, is that Jesus was born in Bethlehem but lived in Nazareth. Luke makes this come about by relating that the Roman emperor Augustus called for a worldwide census to be taken when a man named Quirinius was governor of Syria. Each male head of household was supposed to go to his ancestral city to be counted. Censuses were periodically taken

The "Heavenly Host"

Angels figure prominently in the Gospel stories of Jesus's birth, appearing to Zechariah, Mary, Joseph, and a band of shepherds. In his book The Hidden Jesus, *Donald Spoto writes about what these supernatural beings brought to the story:*

Biblical writers were after something richer [more descriptive], and "angel of the Lord" is a memorably metaphoric way of explicating divine revelation. The annunciation scenes to Zechariah and to Mary emphasize faith not in magic or side show events, but rather in the divine initiative in bringing John [the Baptist] and Jesus into the world; the extraordinary circumstances of the conceptions proclaim God's direct intervention in history. "No-thing shall be impossible with God" is the message to Mary—just as, generations before, in the book of Genesis, God overturned every expectation when the wife of the patriarch Abraham conceived in her advanced age.

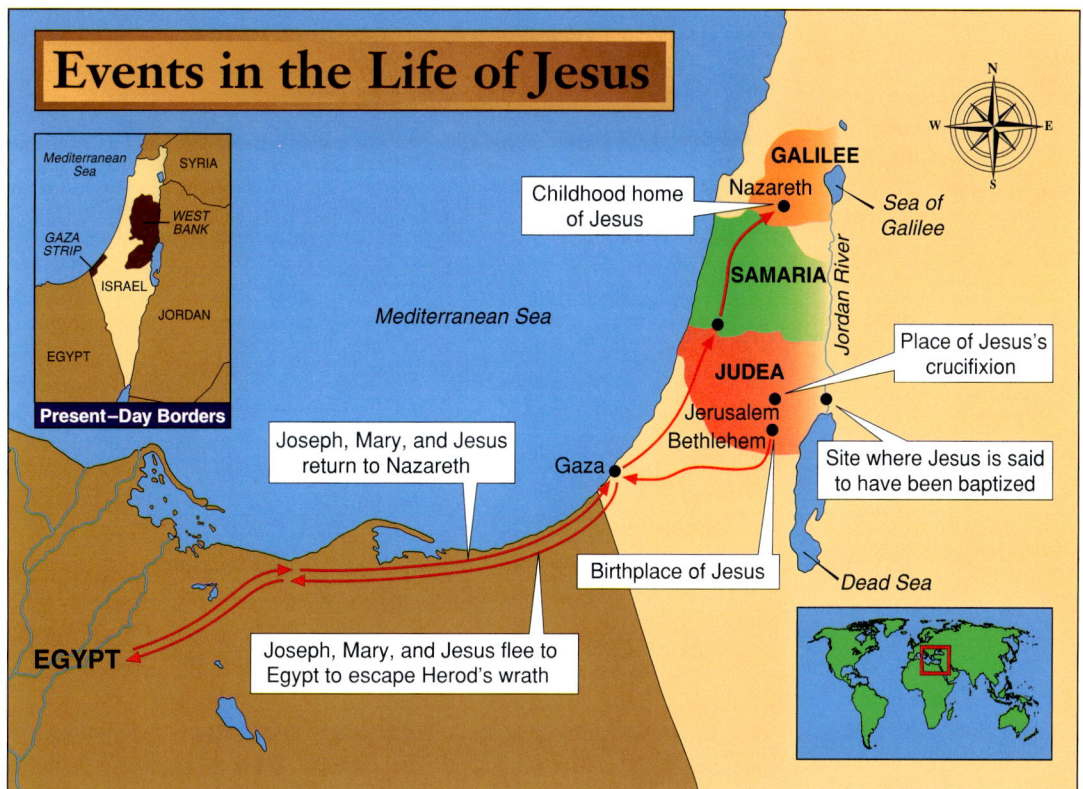

by the Romans, primarily for taxation purposes. One, in fact, did take place in Palestine in about 8 B.C. There is no record, however, that such a wholesale movement of people, which would have caused considerable economic disruption, was involved.

Luke writes that the census forced Joseph to take Mary, by now almost ready to give birth, from Nazareth to Bethlehem, since he was of the lineage of David. There being no room for them in the inn, they took refuge elsewhere. No stable is mentioned, and the depiction of a stable in Nativity scenes stems from Luke's statement that, after Jesus was born, he was put in a manger, a trough for livestock feed.

The Gnostic Version

However, at least two Gnostic Gospels—James and another purported version of Matthew—say that Jesus was born in a cave near Bethlehem. Only after three days, according to "Pseudo-Matthew," did Mary place the baby in a stable, so as to fulfill another prophecy.

In these Gnostic stories, Mary was alone during the birth, but was shortly thereafter attended by midwives brought

The Star of Bethlehem

One of the staples of the story of Jesus's birth is the Star of Bethlehem, which, according to Matthew, led the three magi, also sometimes called kings or wise men, to the manger where the infant lay. Many people have suspected that Matthew's story was invented in order to reinforce the idea of Jesus's divinity.

However, in her article "The Star of Bethlehem: An Astronomical and Historical Perspective," amateur astronomer Susan S. Carroll speculates that the story might be based on actual astronomical events.

In her scenario, the planet Jupiter, named for the king of the Roman gods, formed a conjunction—seeming to come together in the sky—with the star Regulus, the "king star," on August 12, 3 B.C. This foretold a royal birth and alerted the magi. Then, on June 17, 2 B.C., a conjunction of Jupiter and Venus convinced them to start seeking this new king.

According to Carroll, the "star" the magi followed was Jupiter, which, because of the nearness of the winter solstice, shortest day of the year, would have appeared to stand still for six days starting on December 25, 2 B.C. Most experts think this date too late for Jesus's birth, but Carroll speculates on many possibilities, including that when the magi reached Jesus, he was a toddler, not an infant. The article is found at www.sciastro.net/portia/articles/thestar.htm.

---

by Joseph. They marveled that a virgin had borne a son and even examined her to make sure. One of the women suffered an injured hand for daring to touch Mary in doubt, but it was healed when the midwife touched the baby Jesus.

Luke moves immediately from the birth of Jesus to a nearby hillside where shepherds were tending sheep. An angel told the shepherds that "to you is born this day in the city of David a Savior, who is Christ the Lord" (2:11). They rushed off to see for themselves. Why would such a momentous announcement have been made to shepherds, people considered near the bottom of the social scale of the time? One of Luke's primary themes is that Jesus was sent to earth for all people—Jew and gentile, rich and poor. He probably used shepherds to exemplify the latter.

In Matthew's Gospel, the announcement is made to a much different audience—three magi, or "wise men," probably from Parthia. The magi were members of a priestly class that had once dominated the Persian empire and were still highly influential in Jesus's time. They were not magicians or sorcerers. Rather, their religion depended a great deal on astrology—the effect of stars and planets on earthly occurrences—and on the interpretation of dreams.

Although those who sought the baby Jesus are referred to as "three kings," there is no evidence that they were kings or even that there were three of them. The number has been assumed because of the three gifts described—gold and the aromatic resins frankincense and myrrh.

The Magi

Matthew's account of the magi allows him to solve the Bethlehem-Nazareth problem. The magi saw a new star, perhaps a comet or an alignment of planets, signaling to them that a great king had been born. They knew it to be a king of the Jews, possibly from a prophecy that "a scepter shall spring up from Israel" (Numbers 24:17). They came to Judea and asked the king, Herod the Great, where the new king had been born so that they might worship him. The crafty Herod, knowing that the Messiah was supposed to be born in Bethlehem and fearing a threat to his power, sent the magi there, instructing them to find the child and "report to me, so that I, too, may come and worship Him" (Matthew 2:8).

After the magi found Jesus in Bethlehem and presented their rich gifts, they did not return to Herod, being warned by an angel in a dream to return to their homeland by another route. When Herod realized he had been foiled, he sent his soldiers to Bethlehem with orders to kill every male

In this Italian painting, the three magi pay homage to the infant Jesus, bearing gifts of gold and frankincense and myrrh.

child under two years old. There is no record anywhere else of this episode, known as the Slaughter of the Innocents. The author may have inserted it for two reasons. First, it fulfilled yet another prophecy, this one by Jeremiah. Second, it provided a parallel with the story of Moses, in which the Egyptian pharaoh ordered male infants killed. Matthew thus shows, writes John Dominic Crossan, that "Jesus is the new and greater Moses."[8]

The same angel who appeared to the magi in a dream, however, also appeared to Joseph and warned him to take Mary and the baby Jesus and flee to Egypt. They remained there until Herod died, at which

A sixteenth-century painting shows the Holy Family stopping to rest on their flight to Egypt.

time the angel again appeared to Joseph, telling him that it was safe to return. When Joseph reached Palestine, however, he was warned in yet another dream not to return to Judea, where Herod's son Archelaus ruled, but to go to Galilee. Joseph did so, taking up residence in Nazareth.

The Date of Jesus's Birth

Assuming the flight to Egypt was immediate, the visit of the magi probably would have taken place several days, even weeks, after Jesus's birth if it is to be reconciled with Luke's account of Jesus being taken to the Temple in Jerusalem forty days after his birth to dedicate him to God, as was required of every firstborn son, and for a ceremony of purification. This is only one of many problems, however, involved in trying to date Jesus's birth.

The traditional date for Jesus's birth is December 25 in the year that, in the Christian calendar, separates B.C. (before Christ) from A.D. (the Latin *anno Domini*, or in the year of the Lord). If either Matthew or Luke is correct in his account, both the day and year are highly unlikely. In the first place, December nights are cold near Bethlehem. Flocks of sheep would have been kept penned up, not—as Luke writes—in a field in which there would have been little for them to eat at that time of winter anyway.

The year presents more difficulties. If Matthew is correct about Herod's role, Jesus could not have been born after 4 B.C., the well-documented date of Herod's death. If Luke is correct about the Roman census and the Roman official Quirinius, the birth would have taken place in A.D. 6. But this would have been too late, since the gospels say that Jesus was about thirty years old when he began his ministry. The Roman governor Pontius Pilate's tenure ended in A.D. 36.

There was, however, another census in Palestine about 8 B.C., although this was too early for Quirinius to have been involved. Thus, if Matthew is correct about Herod and Luke about a census, Jesus's birth would have been about 7 B.C.

One cannot overemphasize, however, that the Gospel authors—both canonical and noncanonical—neither sought nor especially desired historical accuracy. Their mission was to explain who Jesus was to the people of their time, combining tradition and prophecy within the framework of their own strong beliefs.

It may be that somewhere within the Nativity stories are forces that helped to shape the adult Jesus, particularly if Mary and Joseph had some awareness of what he was destined to become. The other influences would come later, after the family had left either Bethlehem or Egypt and settled in the Galilean village of Nazareth where Jesus would grow to manhood.

Chapter 2

Nazareth

The village of Nazareth was so little regarded by its neighbors that a man who would become one of Jesus's disciples once asked derisively if anything good could come from there. It was, indeed, about as insignificant a spot as could be found in the Roman Empire—an obscure village in a remote area of a distant and largely ignored province. Yet it was here that Jesus is thought to have spent the formative years leading to his ministry.

The historical record of Nazareth is so scant that some scholars formerly doubted its existence in Jesus's time. It is not mentioned in the long list of Palestinian towns in the Old Testament Book of Joshua, nor in the lists of Galilean cities given by the Jewish historian Josephus and in the Talmud, a collection of ancient Jewish writings. Archaeologists have confirmed, however, that people lived at the site as long ago as 2000 B.C.

In New Testament times, however, Nazareth was literally off the beaten path. Two roads passed nearby—the ancient Via Maris caravan route from the Mediterranean to Damascus and another road used by Roman soldiers marching from the Mediterranean to the area south of the Sea of Galilee, which is actually not a sea, but a freshwater lake fed by the Jordan River as it flows south through the Great Rift Valley toward the Dead Sea. Although the roads ran close by, Nazareth was not a good stopping point. First, it sits high on a hillside above the Jezreel Valley. Second, it has only a single spring and thus a limited supply of fresh water.

The lack of abundant water would have limited the village's growth, and scientists have estimated that, in Jesus's time, Nazareth would have housed about three hundred people in thirty-five houses spread over 6 acres (2.4ha). They probably lived, for the most part, a life of quiet solitude.

Galilee

While Nazareth might have been quiet and peaceful, Galilee was not. This northern region of Palestine, even though far removed from the capital at Jerusalem, was notorious as a hotbed of religious fervor and political activism. The clash of cultures—Hellenistic and Jewish—was more pronounced here than anywhere else in the region. Galilee's position on a major trade route had brought both wealth and an influx of non-Jews. New cities, complete with Roman temples and baths, had sprung up around the Sea of Galilee, and the area was far more cosmopolitan than Judea to the south.

Galilee's worldly nature caused the religious hierarchy in Jerusalem to view its inhabitants as people hardly Jews, notoriously lax in their keeping of the Law, as the first five books of the Old Testament were known. On the other hand, however, many Galileans were so fervent in their opposition to foreign gods that they joined the Zealots, a radical sect of Judaism that employed terrorism and assassination against both the Romans and the Jews who cooperated with them.

Shortly after Herod's death in 4 B.C., the Zealots led an uprising in Galilee. It was brutally crushed by the Romans, who destroyed the capital city of Sepphoris and crucified two thousand Jews. Later, about A.D. 6, another revolt broke out, this time in reaction to the ordering of a Roman census, probably the same one referred to in Luke's Gospel. It could have been shortly afterward, according to some of the Gospels, that Joseph, Mary, and the young Jesus returned from Egypt.

The New Testament relates only one incident between Jesus's birth and the journey to Egypt. According to Jewish law, a woman was "unclean" for seven days after giving birth to a male child; she then had to undergo a rite of purification. In Luke's Gospel, Mary and Joseph went to the Temple in Jerusalem to perform this ceremony and also to dedicate the baby Jesus to God, as was required of a firstborn son.

Mary, Joseph, and Jesus return to Judea from Egypt after the death of King Herod. The family settled in the Galilean town of Nazareth.

Jesus and the Cynics

Given Jesus's upbringing in the family of a carpenter in a rural Palestinian town, it seems doubtful that he would have been influenced by any of the Hellenistic, or Greek-based, philosophies of the time. Some experts think, however, that he may have somehow been linked to a group of philosophers known as the Cynics.

The Cynics, followers of the philosopher Diogenes, were known for their pointed, uncompromising attacks on societal norms. Their name comes from the Greek word for "dog." They challenged the status quo, wandering from place to place as itinerant preachers, frequently being expelled or jailed.

While the lifestyle and teachings of Jesus paralleled those of the Cynics in many ways—renunciation of material wealth, living a moral life—there were important differences. The Cynics rejected most forms of religion entirely and performed no miracles or exorcisms.

The Cynic movement, founded in about 440 B.C., was still active in the Roman Empire, including Palestine, at the time of Jesus.

Simeon

At the Temple, they encountered a very elderly man named Simeon, who had been promised that he would not die before laying eyes on the promised Messiah. Simeon took Jesus in his arms and said, "Lord, now let thou thy servant depart in peace, according to thy word; for mine eyes have seen thy salvation which thou hast prepared in the presence of all peoples, a light for revelation to the Gentiles, and for glory to thy people Israel" (2:29–32).

Stories similar to that of Simeon are found elsewhere in the ancient world, and the author of Luke might well have been aware of them. For instance, in the Hindu epic, the *Bhagavad Gita*, an elderly prophet named Asita says he can die happily because he has witnessed the coming of the god Krishna.

How long the family might have remained in Egypt is uncertain. Some Biblical scholars think that Jesus might have been as old as two when the family made the journey from Judea. Others think it took place just a few weeks after his birth. Most agree that he was about three years old when the family returned to Palestine.

Matthew's Gospel gives no details of the time spent in Egypt, but a Gnostic document known as the Arabic Infancy Gospel describes various miracles performed along the way. Many involve water in which the baby Jesus was washed being used to cure people of everything from leprosy to demonic possession. On another occasion, the family was captured by two robbers, one of whom took pity on them and convinced his comrade to release them. The infant Jesus then told Mary that these same robbers, thirty years in the future, would be put to death alongside him.

Return from Egypt

Other noncanonical Gospels, such as Pseudo-Matthew, are full of such stories, considered by the men who compiled the Bible to be more like fairy tales than anything divinely inspired. In addition, these writings emphasize Jesus's divine nature to

Simeon holds the baby Jesus outside the Temple in Jerusalem in this Italian painting. Simeon had been told he would not die until he saw the Jewish Messiah.

the diminution of his human side and thus were excluded from the canon. They do, however, follow Matthew in that Joseph was finally told in a dream that King Herod was dead and that it was safe to return to Palestine.

Matthew and the Gnostic Gospels say that Joseph returned from Egypt to Judea, but decided to move on to Galilee because he feared that Herod's successor, Archelaus, might still pose a danger to Jesus. Why Nazareth? Luke's Gospel says that Nazareth was Joseph's home all along, but he may have picked the small village because of the safety offered by its insignificance.

Moreover, there would have been work nearby. Joseph was identified in the original Greek version of the Bible as a *tekton*. The word has usually been translated as "carpenter," but such a man was actually more of a builder, somewhat like a general contractor today. While there might have been some work for him to do in Nazareth, it is possible that he chose to live there because the city of Sepphoris, only 4 miles (6.4km) away, was being rebuilt after its destruction by the Romans.

Certainly he could not have stayed employed full-time in Nazareth. There would have been only limited use for his talents in houses constructed mostly of clay mixed with straw. These houses usually consisted of a single room and had flat roofs that could serve either as work spaces or, in good weather, for sleeping. Some of the houses were built over small natural caves that were used both as living quarters and for storage. The presence of these subterranean rooms may have given rise to the story that Jesus was born in a cave.

Life in Nazareth

Nazareth was an agricultural community, some aspects of which may be reflected in the imagery of Jesus's later teaching. The people raised sheep and goats on a small scale, but the chief industry was growing grapes, on terraces cut from the hillside, and making wine. Archaeologists digging on the grounds of a hospital in the center of modern Nazareth in 1997 discovered a large basin cut into the native limestone. They concluded that it was used for squashing grapes, the juice from which was collected in vats below. They also found the bases of what they think were towers where guards stood to protect the fields against thieves. If normal customs were followed in ancient Nazareth, everyone—Jesus, Joseph, and Mary included—would have taken part in harvesting and processing the grapes.

Jesus's family, however, was not limited to his father and mother. Mark's Gospel specifically names four brothers—James, Joseph, Judas, and Simon—and says that there also were sisters. Paul's letters also mention Jesus's brothers, one of whom—James—was an early leader of the Christian community in Jerusalem.

Jesus's siblings pose a problem for many Christians. Their existence contradicts the traditional belief that Mary remained a virgin after Jesus's birth. Some have claimed

Josephus's Account

The only historical Jewish mention of Jesus other than the Gospels is found in the writings of historian Flavius Josephus. It is in Book 18, Chapter 3 of his Antiquities of the Jews *and is found in* The Works of Flavius Josephus *at www.ccel.org/j/josephus/works/ant-18.htm:*

Now there was about this time Jesus, a wise man, if it be lawful to call him a man; for he was a doer of wonderful works, a teacher of such men as receive the truth with pleasure. He drew over to him both many of the Jews and many of the Gentiles. He was [the] Christ. And when Pilate, at the suggestion of the principal men amongst us, had condemned him to the cross, those that loved him at the first did not forsake him; for he appeared to them alive again the third day; as the divine prophets had foretold these and ten thousand other wonderful things concerning him. And the tribe of Christians, so named from him, are not extinct at this day.

---

that these siblings may have been Joseph's children by a previous marriage. No such marriage is mentioned in the Old Testament, but other gospels claim that Joseph was ninety years old at the time of Jesus's birth and that his children accompanied him and Mary from Nazareth to Bethlehem. Other people claim that Jesus's brothers and sisters actually were cousins, but the ancient Greek text specifically uses the words *adelphoi* (brothers) and *adelphai* (sisters) instead of *anepsios* (cousin).

Apocryphal Stories

The New Testament is almost completely silent as to Jesus's early childhood. Several curious stories, however, are found in the apocryphal Gospels, most of them probably growing out of oral tradition and becoming more fanciful with each generation. Only one involves an interaction with one of his siblings. Joseph supposedly sent James, his oldest son, to gather wood or vegetables, depending on which Gospel one reads. When a poisonous snake bit James on the hand, Jesus rushed to him and blew on the hand. James was promptly cured, and the snake died. The story may represent Jesus overcoming evil, represented by the snake, much as in the story of Adam, Eve, and the Garden of Eden.

Other apocryphal stories, however, do not portray Jesus in such a favorable light. In these tales, he comes across as a mischievous, somewhat vengeful little boy who is often

The young Jesus carries a plank in this illustration. Although the Bible says almost nothing about Jesus's boyhood, some non-biblical accounts portray him as a carpenter.

careless with his supernatural powers. Both the Infancy Gospel of Thomas and the Gospel of Pseudo-Matthew relate an incident when Jesus was four or five years old. Playing by a stream, he made seven pools of clay on the bank, then commanded the water from the stream to run into the pools and back out again.

In Pseudo-Matthew's version, another boy standing nearby took a stick and destroyed the channels between the stream and Jesus's pools. Jesus grew angry and said, "Dost thou destroy the works which I have wrought?" The boy promptly dropped dead. Only when Mary protested did Jesus, reluctantly, kick "the hinder parts of the dead boy"[9] and bring him back to life.

Not all of Jesus's supposed playmates were so fortunate. In a story from the Thomas Gospel, Jesus was jostled by another boy as he walked through Nazareth. Jesus rebuked the boy, who fell lifeless to the ground. When the boy's parents complained to Joseph, they were struck blind.

Stories Excluded

The apocryphal Gospels are full of stories in which the boy Jesus performs wonders—bringing clay birds to life, carrying water to Mary in a handkerchief that miraculously does not leak, getting a bumper crop of wheat to grow from a few handfuls planted. Such tales probably were created by writers who, with some knowledge of what Jesus supposedly did as an adult, assumed he must have exhibited such powers as a child. The idea of Jesus as a sometimes naughty little boy, however, was not one the early Christian leaders thought suitable for the Bible.

Jesus's actual childhood was probably similar to that of any small boy in a rural Palestinian town. If all his siblings were, indeed, Joseph's by an earlier marriage, he would have been the baby of the family, probably cared for by his older sisters as Mary went about her household chores. When he was old enough, about nine or ten, he would have started helping Joseph in his work.

It was traditional in most Jewish families for sons to follow their fathers' occupations. Mark's Gospel, indeed, refers to Jesus as "the carpenter" (6:3). The only accounts of Jesus's carpentry, however, appear in the apocryphal Gospels and are just as fanciful as the other childhood stories. According to the Arabic Infancy Gospel, "Joseph was not very skillful in carpentry."[10] He did not need to be. Anytime he mismeasured a piece of wood, all Jesus had to do was stretch out his hand and the wood became the desired length.

Trouble at School

The apocryphal Gospels treat Jesus's education in much the same way, seeming to relish the trials of unfortunate schoolmasters trying to teach a boy who already knows everything. According to Pseudo-Matthew, when a teacher named Zachyas offered to instruct Jesus, the five-year-old

Carpenter or Scholar?

Tradition has it that Jesus's father Joseph was a carpenter and that Jesus may have followed that trade, as well, as was customary for Jews in first-century Palestine. Colin Cross, in his book Who Was Jesus?, *writes that the image of a working-class Jesus should not be taken too far:*

It is simply not sufficient to write off most of his [Jesus's] life by sentimentalising him as a carpenter thinking up great truths while labouring in his workshop: even the gospels, taken literally, make no such claim. When he returned to Nazareth and started preaching it seems to have been after an absence and people had to exercise their memories to recall that he was the carpenter's son. The carpenter theory is inherently improbable because it is not the way that great ideas can be expected to come. Moreover, Jesus's teachings reflect a sophisticated knowledge of the Jewish thought of his day and this must have come from careful, intelligent study.

---

boy said, "Thou who readest the law, and art learned in it, bidest in the law; but I was before the law. But since thou thinkest that no one is equal to thee in learning, thou shalt be taught by me."[11]

At length, Jesus agreed to attend a synagogue school taught by an elderly scholar named Levi. When the teacher started him out with the first letter of the alphabet, however, Jesus quickly ran through the entire alphabet, ascribing multiple meanings to each letter. "I cannot withstand the words of this child," Levi moaned. "I shall now flee from this town, because I cannot understand them."[12]

Even so, Levi was more fortunate than another, unnamed teacher recorded in the Arabic Infancy Gospel. When this man ordered Jesus to pronounce the first letter of the alphabet, Jesus remained silent. The schoolmaster angrily hit him on the head with a stick, whereupon the teacher was struck dead.

Jesus's actual education would have been the same as for any Jewish boy of the time. The Jews valued education highly, and Galileans seem to have been exceptionally scholarly. Experts say that the writings of first-century Galilean scholars are more numerous and of higher quality than those from Judea.

Jewish Education

According to the New Testament, Nazareth, small as it was, had a synagogue—the Jewish place of worship that also served as a school. Classes were divided between the *bet sefer*, or elementary school, and the *bet midrash*, or secondary school. Limits were placed on the number of students per teacher, with twenty-five the upper limit.

Starting at about age five, boys began to learn to read so that they would be able to read the Torah (another name for the first five books of the Old Testament) in the synagogue at the time of their bar mitzvah, or coming-of-age ceremony. They learned from the Torah and from other sacred writings. Textbooks were unknown, and the long scrolls on which the scriptures were written were expensive since each had to be copied by hand. It would have been surprising if a village as small as Nazareth had a complete set of Torah scrolls, but some could have been borrowed from neighboring towns.

A Jewish boy's education involved not only reading the scriptures, but thoroughly memorizing them. Since the scrolls were scarce or even altogether unavailable, memorization was the key to learning. The teacher would recite passages, either reading from a scroll or working from memory, and the boys would repeat after him. According to modern-day Jewish scholar Shmuel Safrai, "There is the frequent expression, 'the chirping of children,' which was heard by people passing close by a synagogue as the children were reciting a verse. . . . It was frequently advised not to learn in a whisper, but aloud. This was the only way to overcome the danger of forgetting."[13]

Such recitations were supposed to continue outside the synagogue while the boys went about their daily chores. Students were encouraged to take every opportunity, while tending a flock or a garden, for instance, to recite either aloud or under their breath. Pausing even to exclaim on the beauty of a tree or a bird was, according to the Talmud tradition, an affront to God.

Knowledge of Scripture

Consequently, Jewish males had a profound knowledge of scripture. "The Scriptures were known to everyone," writes Professor Safrai. "From quite early in the Second Temple period [536 B.C. to A.D. 70], one could hardly find a little boy in the street who didn't know the Scriptures."[14]

Certainly this was true of Jesus, judging from what is written about him in the New Testament. Time after time, he would counter those using scriptural quotations to challenge one of his actions or teachings with equally or more valid quotations from other sources. No one ever got the better of him in any such disagreement.

Jesus's exceptional scholarship was evident in the single event of his boyhood related in the New Testament. The author of Luke says that when Jesus was twelve years old, his parents went, as they had each year, to the Temple in Jerusalem at the holy time of Passover, which commemorated God's freeing of the Israelites from slavery in Egypt centuries before. As

Mary and Joseph were returning to Nazareth, they realized that Jesus was not with them. This is not as unusual as it may sound, since they were probably traveling with many other families from Nazareth and thought that Jesus was with friends or relatives.

When they returned to Jerusalem, they finally found Jesus—three days later—in the Temple "sitting among the teachers, listening to them and asking them questions; and all who heard him were amazed at his understanding and his answers" (Luke 2:46–47). When Mary admonished her son for worrying his parents, Jesus replied, "How is it that you sought me? Did you not know that I must be in my Father's house?" (2:49).

At the age of twelve, Jesus discusses scripture with the elders of the Temple in Jerusalem.

Jesus's answer seems logical given the notion that the Holy Spirit, not Joseph, was his true father, but the Gospel says that Mary and Joseph did not understand what Jesus was saying to them. It would be puzzling if they did not, given that, in Matthew's and Luke's Gospels respectively, Joseph and Mary had been specifically told the nature of the child.

Jesus in the Temple

After this episode, the New Testament Gospels fall silent as to Jesus's youth, Luke saying only that he "increased in wisdom and in stature, and in favor with God and man" (2:52). What he did between the ages of twelve and thirty, when he is supposed to have begun his ministry, is a complete blank. Even the apocryphal Gospels are silent, the Arabic Infancy Gospel saying only that Jesus "began to hide His miracles and mysteries and secrets, and to give attention to the Law, until he completed his thirtieth year."[15]

During this time he probably worked alongside his father, continued to study the scriptures and, highly unusual for a Jewish man, did not marry. At some point, however, it is thought that he began to depart from the Judaism of the day, possibly under the guidance of the man who was to be a primary influence in his life—his cousin John the Baptist. How long or how well they knew one another, or even if they met at all prior to Jesus's baptism at John's hands, are matters for speculation. The New Testament Gospels agree, however, that the baptism was the turning point in Jesus's life. He might have had an ordinary Jewish upbringing, but from this point on he was to be anything but ordinary.

Chapter 3

The Jordan

If the miracle stories of Jesus's childhood can be dismissed—and there is no absolute assurance that they can—then he had a fairly normal upbringing for his place and time. About all that can be gleaned from the New Testament is that he learned carpentry from his earthly father and absorbed a thorough grounding in Jewish scriptures. What, then, led him at age thirty to embark on the life of an itinerant preacher?

He may have had some sense of great purpose, perhaps imparted to him by his mother if the Nativity accounts are true. But why would he have waited until what was then considered almost middle age to act on that feeling? What were the forces that impelled him? The Gospels give a clue by linking the start of Jesus's ministry to his baptism in the Jordan River by John the Baptist.

The emphasis the Gospels place on this event underscores the importance of John in Jesus's life and in his decision to give up what was probably a quiet, comfortable existence in Nazareth. In fact, John's influence on Jesus was very likely much more profound than the Gospels suggest. It is possible that John—and Jesus—were members of a radical Jewish sect that shaped their teachings.

According to the Nativity story in Luke's Gospel, John was born about six months before Jesus. His mother, Elizabeth, was a cousin of Mary, and it was to Elizabeth that Mary revealed her visit from the angel. Luke's mention of John leaping for joy in Elizabeth's womb on hearing Mary's voice has been interpreted as the first of many passages intended to put John in a subordinate role to Jesus.

John's Birth

It is clear from Luke's story, however, that John was given great stature by the early Christians. In some ways, his birth is

Although the Bible mentions no childhood relationship between Jesus and John the Baptist, this painting depicts John holding the infant Jesus.

The Holy Spirit

The Gospels frequently mention the Holy Spirit. Some theologians believe that Jesus was made the Messiah, which means "anointed," at his baptism. Then, according to Luke, "the Holy Spirit descended upon him in bodily form, as a dove, and a voice came from heaven, 'Thou art my beloved Son; with thee I am well pleased'" (3:22).

More than one hundred years after Jesus's death, the idea grew up that there are three aspects to God. This concept, known as the Holy Trinity, was rooted in Matthew's Gospel, in which Jesus told the Apostles to "go therefore and make disciples of all nations, baptizing them in the name of the Father and of the Son and of the Holy Spirit" (28:19). One early theologian, Tertullian, explained this Holy Trinity by writing that God exists in three persons but is also one person made up of three substances.

The idea of the Holy Spirit and how it is or is not one with Jesus and God has been the subject of scholarly debate—and occasionally nonscholarly sectarian violence—throughout history. While most Christian churches accept the idea of God in three persons, some, such as the Unitarians and Jehovah's Witnesses, say that the Holy Spirit is God's force or will, but not part of God. And the Church of Jesus Christ of Latter-day Saints, known as the Mormons, contends that the Holy Spirit is a separate entity altogether.

---

almost as miraculous as that of Jesus. Gabriel, the same angel who appeared to Mary, also appeared to John's father, Zechariah. The angel told Zechariah that his son's name would be John and that "he will be great before the Lord, and he shall drink no wine nor strong drink, and he will be filled with the Holy Spirit, even from his mother's womb" (1:15). The key difference, of course, is that while John, according to the angel, was to be filled with the Holy Spirit, Jesus was to be conceived by the power of the Holy Spirit.

The angel went on to say that John would be a mighty prophet who would have many followers. He added, however, that John's role would be to prepare the way for someone greater.

Luke further emphasizes John's role as a messenger from God by saying that the angel told Zechariah that he would remain unable to speak until John's birth. When at last Zechariah was able to speak, his first words were to prophesy to the newborn baby that "you, child, will be called the prophet of the Most High; for you will go before the Lord to prepare his ways" (1:76).

The tradition of a strong relationship between Jesus and John the Baptist is evident in the New Testament Gospels. John appears as a prophet at the very start of the Gospels of Mark and John. In Matthew and Luke, John appears immediately after the Nativity stories. The wording in each version is much the same, indicating a common source. Matthew's is typical: "In those days came John the Baptist, preaching in the wilderness of Judea, 'Repent, for the kingdom of heaven is at hand'" (3:1–2).

The Wilderness

In the Gospels, John suddenly appeared out of the wilderness. There is no indication of any prior ministry. Indeed, there is no mention of John at all subsequent to Luke's story of his birth. The words "wilderness of Judea," however, are a clue to who and what John the Baptist may have been.

It was in this same area south of Jerusalem, known as Qumran, that in 1947 a shepherd boy exploring a cave discovered ceramic pots containing fragments of scrolls. Known as the Dead Sea Scrolls, they are thought by most experts to have been the work of a radical Jewish sect known as the Essenes. The sect is thought to date to about 175 B.C. when a group of priests, disturbed by what they felt to be a move toward Hellenism and away from traditional Judaism, withdrew and formed their own community. They were both eschatological, looking toward the imminent end of the world, and apocalyptic, foreseeing the end of the world in terms of widespread doom and devastation.

The Essenes were extreme ascetics, neither eating meat nor drinking wine. They were almost exclusively male, and they encouraged celibacy. To replenish their numbers, they adopted male children, although some communities seem to have brought in women for procreation purposes. They owned no personal property, holding everything in common.

Similarities abound between the writings contained in the Dead Sea Scrolls and the teachings of John the Baptist and Jesus. Both treat the Holy Spirit as an aspect of God, a concept seldom found in the Judaic tradition. Likewise, both emphasize the forces of "light" and "dark" and both refer to what would come after the end of the world as the "kingdom of God."

Similarities in Scripture

The most striking similarity between the Dead Sea Scrolls and the New Testament is a statement in the former that the Messiah will be "he who liberates the captives, restores sight to the blind, straightens the bent . . . [will] revive the dead and bring good news to the poor."[16] Early in Jesus's ministry, he repeats this line almost word for word in answer to a question from John.

Such parallels have led to speculation that John, and perhaps even Jesus, were members of the Essene community. The evidence is stronger for John, mainly because of his use of water in the rite known as baptism. Ritual cleansing had long been part of religions throughout the world, frequently in regard to sexual activity, childbirth, and menstruation. So, too, had the idea of death and rebirth into a new life, as in Buddhism.

The Essenes employed ritual baths as acts of purification, washing frequently in cold water. There is no indication, however, that the water was supposed, in any way, to wash a person's sins away, as it did in baptism. In order for the rite to have meaning, a person must have repented, or felt remorse for, any sins. With repentance, both John and Jesus taught, came God's forgiveness, thus cleansing the soul. The subsequent baptism, then, was a consecration and rededication of the body.

John was certainly, like the Essenes, an ascetic. Mark says that he was "clothed with camel's hair, and had a leather girdle around his waist, and ate locusts and wild honey" (1:6). But there were important differences. The Essenes withdrew into their own communities, shunning the outside world. John went freely among the people, including those the Essenes would deem unclean, exhorting them to repent. The baptism performed by John could be a one-time event in a person's life, whereas the Essenes' rites were almost daily.

John the Baptist advised his disciples to repent their sins and prepare for the coming of the Jewish messiah.

John and Jesus

Despite such differences, it seems to most experts that John the Baptist was at one time a part of the Qumran community but had left and struck out on his own, carrying a similar, but slightly different message. What, then, was the relationship of Jesus to the Essenes, if any, and to John prior to the baptism in the Jordan?

Some experts think that Jesus himself might have been an Essene, and some present-day, self-styled Essenes adamantly believe so. The similarities in phrases and in basic religious doctrine would suggest such a possibility, and some writers have even referred to Christianity as "Essenism popularized."[17]

Most authorities, however, while they admit the parallels, say that the differences are too great. Although Jesus never, as far as is known, married, his lifestyle, though simple, was far from the rigid asceticism practiced by the Essenes and even much more liberal than that of John. He ate meat, drank wine, and made it a point to associate with people from all levels of society. His message was much more one of peace and love than doom and destruction.

A much stronger case can be made that Jesus's religious outlook was heavily influenced by the Essenes. Colin Cross writes that "the safer view is that Jesus and the early Christians were profoundly influenced by them [the Essenes] . . . but that in the last analysis Jesus was an independent teacher with doctrines of his own."[18] Perhaps much of the influence came secondhand through Jesus's relationship with John. Exactly what that relationship was, however, is a matter of debate. The Gospels treat the meeting between the two cousins as if it were a brief, although highly significant event.

The Baptism

John, by this time, had attracted a large following. Matthew writes that "Jerusalem and all Judea and all the region about the

The Charisma of Jesus

Although Jesus's message had great appeal as he preached it to the people of Galilee, part of his popularity was also probably due to his style of teaching. As John Drane writes in *Son of Man*, "To put it simply, Jesus was more appealing than many of the other religious leaders of his day. The Pharisees were bookish people . . . but he [Jesus] was unashamedly a populariser. He had no difficulty attracting substantial crowds wherever he went."

Most writers, however, are quick to add that his teachings would not have had near the impact, and might not even have survived, without the miracles intended to show that his inspiration came from God. Indeed, without the miracles, writes Donald Spoto in *The Hidden Jesus*, "Jesus of Nazareth becomes Jesus of Nashville, a nice, unthreatening bumpkin who brings a simple little country message about love to slick urbanites and —in one of the worst clichés of our time—makes us feel good about ourselves."

John baptizes Jesus in this Italian painting. The cross in John's hand foreshadows the crucifixion, while the dove at the top symbolizes the Holy Spirit.

Jordan" (3:5) came to him to be baptized. It is at this point that Jesus came from Galilee to be baptized. The Gospels do not say if the two men knew one another. It would have been odd, since they were cousins, if they did not. On the other hand, it could have been that Jesus, feeling the need for some sort of spiritual renewal, went south to hear this prophet of whom the entire nation was talking.

What the Gospels do say is that when John saw Jesus coming to be baptized, John knew that this was the person whose coming had been foretold. In John 1:30, he says, "This is he of whom I said, 'After me comes a man who ranks ahead of me because he was before me.'" In other words, John was saying that Jesus's coming had been ordained by God from the beginning of time.

Why Jesus thought it necessary to be baptized by John has puzzled many Christians. Some say that, although Jesus was without sin, he was symbolically taking on the sins of the people he had been sent by God to save. "Probably," writes Professor Barry Smith of Atlantic Baptist University, "Jesus undergoes baptism in order to identify himself vicariously with Israel, even though he himself did not need to repent and be forgiven. Such an identification with Israel is a presupposition of the assumption of his messianic function."[19]

The baptism evidently provided Jesus with the kind of spiritual experience he had sought. The Gospels seek to convey this idea with the story of the heavens opening, a dove descending onto Jesus, and the voice of God proclaiming him to be God's son. Whatever might have happened, it changed

Jesus completely. From now on, he would never return to his former life and family. Hendrikus Boers writes that Jesus's relationship with John "demanded that he make a choice in lifestyle that sheds important light on the kind of person he was."[20]

Jesus as Disciple

Scholars think it is likely, in the words of J.R. Porter, "that Jesus began as a disciple of John the Baptist. John began his work east of the Jordan and Jesus [according to John's Gospel] was with him. No one can say how long this might have been, but eventually Jesus must have felt it necessary to go his own way—to take a course different from that of John."[21]

Many of John's followers thought that he was the promised Messiah. This belief endured long after his death. Paul, in his travels about A.D. 50, recorded encountering John's disciples, and small remnants of the group endured until about A.D. 200. The early Gospel writers knew such a movement existed, considered it a rival to Christianity, and took great pains to diminish John's role. They would not have been likely, for instance, to admit that Jesus was once a follower of John. Instead, they tell the story that Jesus found his calling as a result of his sojourn in the wilderness.

The Gospels say that immediately after the Holy Spirit descended on Jesus, that same spirit either drove or led him, depending on which Gospel one reads, to the "wilderness," east of the Jordan River in present-day Syria or Jordan. Malcolm Muggeridge prefers the "led" version: "It is a natural impulse thus to seek isolation and quiet after an experience which dramatically reshapes and redirects a life."[22] Indeed, it was already a tradition in the ancient world for a person seeking spiritual direction to withdraw from the everyday world, seeking enlightenment through prayer, solitude, and perhaps the kind of visions that could be brought about by fasting and thirst. British army officer T.E. Lawrence, who gained fame during World War I as "Lawrence of Arabia," wrote that Arab holy men retreated to the desert because "in its solitude they heard more certainly the living word they brought with them."[23]

The Temptations

When Jesus went from Judea into the wilderness, he may have already decided that his future was not to be spent as a disciple of John. Rather, his meditation might have been on what his new role was to be and whether or not he was worthy to undertake it. The Gospels present his self-examination as a story of three temptations on the part of Satan—one to turn stones into bread, a second to throw himself from a cliff and call on God to save him, and a third to have complete power over the world in exchange for worshipping Satan. Jesus rejected all three.

In their accounts of the temptations in the desert, the Gospel writers seek to draw a parallel between Jesus and the great Jewish prophet Moses. The final temptation, for instance, reflects the passage in the Book of Exodus in which Moses views Palestine from atop a mountain but is told by God he will not live to enter the land that has been promised. Jesus's rejection of Satan's offer of power, and Satan's subsequent disappearance, suggest that the author—Luke in this case—was making the point that Jesus was greater than Moses.

The tradition of temptation was strong in Jewish writings. Adam and Eve were tempted by a serpent in the Garden of Eden. Abraham was supposed to have faced ten temptations. Such stories may have come from an even older tradition—that of the Egyptian god Horus being taken to a mountaintop to be tempted by his evil brother, Set.

The temptations of Jesus are supposed to have lasted forty days, a clear parallel to the forty years the Israelites wandered in the wilderness after leaving Egypt, the forty days and nights of Noah's flood, and the forty days Moses fasted at Mount Sinai before receiving God's commandments. In each instance, there was a renewal, a new beginning for the Jews. Similarly, the Gospels seem to say, Jesus emerged from the wilderness with a new spirit of purpose.

John's Arrest

On Jesus's return, two important things occurred. First, he began to gather followers of his own. Second, John the Baptist was

---

Jesus and Women

One of the most outrageous practices of Jesus, in the eyes of his opponents, was his association with women who were not members of his own family. As Donald Spoto writes in *The Hidden Jesus*, "It put him in direct and immediate confrontation with prevailing Jewish convention. . . . Women, slaves and children constituted the trio of the disenfranchised in Israel."

Like women in today's very traditional Islamic cultures, Jewish women in Jesus's time were heavily veiled when they went outside the home and were forbidden to speak with men who did not belong to their families.

"It is not going too far to say that his [Jesus's] was the first mission in history that had no gender bias," Spoto continues. "It may also not be going too far to suggest that, in our own time, some of Jesus's most outspoken partisans may not be faithful to his vision. In some Christian churches, for example, women are still very much second-class citizens."

arrested. It is not clear which came first. Matthew, Mark, and Luke claim that Jesus's ministry began after John's arrest, perhaps to explain Jesus going out on his own.

John's Gospel, however, tells a far different story. His account, in which the greatest care is taken to make Jesus superior to John, says that the two men were

Salome receives the head of John the Baptist on a platter. She requested John's head as a reward from Herod Antipas, after dancing for him.

preaching at the same time and that some of John's followers complained that many were going over to Jesus. John replied, "He must increase, but I must decrease" (3:30).

According to the Gospels, John was arrested because of his repeated condemnation of Herod Antipas, son of Herod the Great and tetrarch, or governor, of Galilee. Antipas was in an incestuous relationship with his niece, Herodias, who had been the wife of Antipas's half brother Phillip. When John loudly denounced Herodias as an adulteress, Antipas had him arrested. According to Mark's Gospel, Herodias wanted John killed, but Antipas was fearful of killing a man who he thought was a holy prophet.

Herodias then concocted a scheme whereby her daughter by Phillip, Salome, would so captivate Antipas by a dance that he would grant her any wish. After the dance, Salome requested as her favor the head of John the Baptist. Antipas was horrified, but kept his promise, and John was beheaded, his head being brought to Salome on a silver platter.

The Jewish historian Flavius Josephus gives another version of John's arrest, saying that Antipas "feared lest the great influence John had over the people might put it into his power and inclination to raise a rebellion."[24] This statement provides an insight into the kind of Messiah John's followers believed him to be—a warrior who would overthrow the Romans and restore the lost glory of the kingdom of Israel.

John might have shared this view of the Messiah, which could explain the question he sent from prison to Jesus, who was making a name for himself but whose message was one of peace and love instead of rebellion. John sent two of his followers to Jesus to ask, "Are you he who is to come, or shall we look for another?" (Luke 7:19). Jesus replied with the phrases later discovered in the Dead Sea Scrolls: "Go back and report to John what you hear and see: The blind receive sight, the lame walk, those who have leprosy are cured, the deaf hear, the dead are raised, and the good news is preached to the poor" (Matthew 11:4–5).

The Disciples

After John's death, Jesus's fame began to grow. Instead of being a follower, he was now clearly a leader and began to draw more people to him. Chief among them were the twelve men known as the disciples. They were distinct from other followers in that Jesus specifically sought them out. They were an odd assortment. Four—brothers Simon (later renamed Peter) and Andrew, brothers James the Greater and John—were fishermen. One, Matthew, was a tax collector. A second Simon was a Zealot, a member of the radical sect that believed that the coming of the Messiah would involve armed rebellion. Judas Iscariot, the disciple who eventually would betray Jesus, evidently had some sort of business background because he kept what money the group had and bought supplies.

The Disciples

Although they played a prominent part in the life of Jesus of Nazareth and in the early Christian church, very little is known about most of the twelve men he chose as his disciples. Nothing is known about some of them except their names, and in one case even that is in doubt.

The original twelve disciples were Simon (later named Peter) and his brother Andrew, James the Greater and his brother John, James the Lesser, Thomas, Philip, Bartholomew, Matthew, Simon the Zealot, Judas Iscariot, and a twelfth variously called Thaddeus, Lebbaeus, or Jude.

Jesus had many more disciples. Luke writes that at one point he appointed seventy "disciples," some of them perhaps women, and "sent them on ahead of him, two by two, into every town and place where he himself was about to come" (10:1).

The number twelve, however, had a special significance. As John Dominic Crossan points out in *Jesus: A Revolutionary Biography*, "The point . . . is that Jesus' community forms a New Israel in miniature, a new People of God with twelve new patriarchs to replace the twelve sons of Jacob from the Old Testament."

Jesus washes the feet of one of his disciples in order to underscore the importance of humility.

Almost nothing is known about the remaining five—James the Lesser, Thomas, Thaddeus, Bartholomew, and Philip.

It was common at the time for young men to leave home to study with a famous, established teacher. These disciples, however, were not young, and Jesus was hardly established. "Someone like Jesus who breaks the established patterns of life would have a very difficult time persuading others that he is right to do so," writes theologian Pheme Perkins. "And it certainly must have been difficult for the disciples to accept Jesus' call to break with their own families and occupations to follow him."[25]

Jesus made it clear from the outset that the disciples would be more than mere followers. He expected his disciples to be active participants in his ministry, later calling on them to preach and even perform healings in his name.

The calling of the disciples would turn out to have enormous consequences. Jesus never intended to start a new religion, or, if he did, he never said so. He was a devout Jew, and his message, which he gave to an almost exclusively Jewish audience, was to love God, love others, and obey the Jewish laws. It would be these largely unschooled disciples, along with converts such as Paul, who would expand Jesus's teaching into Christianity.

The Nazarenes' Anger

Jesus's followers did not include, at least at first, his neighbors in Nazareth or members of his own family. According to the Gospels, Jesus attended the Nazareth synagogue and read from Isaiah 61:1–2: "The Spirit of the Lord God is upon me, because the Lord has anointed me to bring good tidings to the afflicted; he has sent me to bind up the brokenhearted, to proclaim liberty to the captives, and the opening of the prison to those who are bound to proclaim the year of the Lord's favor." After finishing, he told the congregation "Today, this scripture has been fulfilled in your hearing" (Luke 4:21).

The Nazarenes were shocked. They asked each other, "Where did this man get this wisdom and these mighty works? Is not this the carpenter's son? . . . Where then did this man get all this?" (Matthew 13:54–56). Jesus answered them, "Prophets are not without honor except in their own country and in their own house" (13:57). At this, the Nazarenes, Luke writes, were so angry that they wanted to throw him from a cliff but had to settle for driving him from the town.

The rejection extended to Jesus's own family, even his mother. One of the great contradictions of the Gospels is that Mary, who according to Luke had been told of her son's powers and destiny, attempted in Mark's account to stop him from preaching. As Jesus's fame spread, the people of Nazareth began to say that this man who had grown up among them had gone out of his mind. When his family heard this, they "went out to restrain him" (Mark 3:21).

Later in Jesus's career, at least some of his family were reconciled to him. Mary became a faithful follower, and Jesus's brother James became one of the great founders of Christianity. For the time being, however, Jesus of Nazareth had been abandoned by his family and rejected by his neighbors. Instilled by his baptism with a sense of mission, focused and strengthened by his ordeal in the wilderness, he gathered a small group of followers and launched a ministry that, although brief, would change the world.

Chapter 4

Galilee

Jesus began his ministry, Luke's Gospel says, when he was thirty years old. For an undetermined period of time—as long as three years or as brief as one—he roamed back and forth across Galilee, always on the move, seldom pausing to rest, pushing himself and his disciples as if he knew his time was limited.

He taught and preached, underscoring his message with acts that were miracles to some, blasphemy to others. He brought comfort to many who heard him, but, to his great frustration, many others refused to heed his message. He also drew the attention of those in authority, arousing envy and jealousy. All wondered if he were the promised Messiah, but Jesus—if, indeed, he himself knew—kept such knowledge to himself.

Jesus's Teaching

The Gospels emphasize Jesus's teaching, the role with which he was probably most comfortable. John takes special care to tell his readers that the disciples called Jesus "'Rabbi' (which means Teacher)" (1:38). His role as a teacher, however, was not consistent with the Jewish concept of the Messiah—a warrior and a king. Thus, it would have been difficult for the people listening to Jesus teach and preach to picture him as their long-promised savior.

His teaching methods were somewhat unorthodox. He had no synagogue or temple, as would have been the usual case with a rabbi or priest well-known enough to attract a following. Instead, he taught wherever he happened to be, either with his chosen disciples or with those who sought him out. His two most famous sermons were outdoors, one on a hill—"the Mount"—and the other on a plain. He preached in synagogues and in the Temple in Jerusalem on occasion, but more often taught from under a tree, by the shore of a lake, or—in one instance—from a boat just offshore.

This painting depicts Jesus preaching to the people of Galilee from a pulpit, but he more often preached in a less formal setting.

Jesus taught, as did most scholars of his time, by discourse, or lecturing, by questioning those in attendance with what theologian John Dominic Crossan calls "an oral brilliance that few of those trained in literate and scribal disciplines can ever attain."[26] Much of the time he taught through parables, stories used to explain or illustrate the point being taught. Jesus used them frequently, but in a manner different from that of most religious teachers. Most people assume that he used parables because he wanted to make complex theological issues more readily understandable to his listeners, most of whom were rural Jewish peasants. According to the Gospels, it was just the opposite.

When teaching his disciples, Jesus talked in terms of God and salvation. When speaking to the masses, he simply

54 *The Importance of Jesus of Nazareth*

told the parable and left his listeners to figure out for themselves what it meant or, more important, to seek him out and ask him. He wanted only the most deeply committed people as his followers. The people who heard the parables had a choice. They could shake their heads in bafflement, dismiss Jesus, and go on their way, or they could ponder what he said, seek him out, and ask him for an explanation. Therefore, the parables were, as biographer Donald Spoto writes, "not merely edifying little stories, they compelled Jesus' hearers to make a decision about him and his mission."[27]

The Kingdom of God

The core of that mission was to preach about the kingdom of God. The term itself would have been familiar to those of Jesus's listeners versed in scripture, but they might not have understood the context in which he used it. Most would have pictured an all-conquering Messiah. Jesus, on the other hand, maintained that the kingdom he described was not physical, but spiritual, and described it in two ways.

One was in terms of the end of the world, when God would judge all humanity and the righteous would exist in the kingdom of God, widely interpreted by Christians to mean a heavenly paradise. Life after death was not traditionally a part of Judaism, but Jesus said specifically that "God so loved the world that he gave his only Son [Jesus], that whoever believes in him should not perish but have eternal life" (John 3:16).

Jesus also described the kingdom of God, however, as "in the midst of you" (Luke 17:21)—a spiritual state of being that people could achieve before any kind of heavenly judgment. This version of the kingdom was open to those who heeded his call to repent their sins and lead righteous lives. The formula, he said in Mark's Gospel, is to love God totally and love others as much as oneself.

As for the ultimate arrival of the kingdom of God, Jesus was unclear as to when it would be. At one point, according to Matthew's Gospel, he said that it would take place within the lifetime of the present generation. It was little wonder, then, that after Jesus's death, his followers expected the final judgment within a short time. Yet in the same passage, Jesus says, "But of that day and hour no one knows, not even the angels of heaven, nor the Son, but the Father only" (Matthew 24:36). For this reason, he tells his disciples, they should maintain a state of readiness.

Jesus gave the most detailed picture of the inhabitants of the kingdom of God in his Sermon on the Mount, which was actually addressed to his disciples, rather than to a crowd. Many scholars, in fact, doubt that he gave such a sermon at all, concluding instead that Matthew and Luke used it as a literary device for reciting many of Jesus's sayings that had been handed down over the years. Either way, it was an eloquent way to set forth his message.

Jesus delivers the Sermon on the Mount in this French painting. According to the Bible, Jesus spoke on the Mount only to his disciples, and not to a crowd of people.

The sermon lists three types of people in the kingdom of heaven. First are those who are powerless and persecuted. Second are people whose place in heaven is assured by their actions on earth—the merciful, the pure in heart, and the peacemakers. Last are those specifically persecuted "on my account. Rejoice and be glad, for your reward is great in heaven" (Matthew 5:11–12).

Barriers to Salvation

Righteousness, however, is not enough on its own to qualify a person for salvation, Jesus taught. In addition, a person must actively seek salvation, sometimes called God's grace, and must prize it above everything and everyone, including family and—especially—material possessions. Jesus considered possessions the most difficult obstacle facing those seeking the kingdom of God. He told his disciples, "It is easier for a camel to go through the eye of a needle than for a rich man to enter the kingdom of God" (Matthew 19:23–24).

Another serious barrier to God's kingdom, in Jesus's view, was pride—a shortcoming that afflicted even his closest followers. The disciples at one point seemed to get the notion that their standing with Jesus on earth would enhance their status in heaven. Luke and Matthew record that the disciples even argued among themselves as to who was the greatest. When Jesus heard their bickering, he placed a child by his side and said, "Truly, I say to you, unless you turn and become like children, you will never enter the kingdom of heaven. Whoever humbles himself like this child, he is the greatest in the kingdom of heaven" (Matthew 18:3–4).

Jesus held out no hope of salvation, however, for those who rejected him. In Matthew 10:32–33, he warned, "Whoever acknowledges me before men, I will also acknowledge him before my Father in heaven. But whoever disowns me before men, I will disown him before my Father in heaven."

Jesus's Healings

One of the points Jesus is said to have made with his healings is that the power of God worked through him. Other aspects, however, such as whom he healed (the poor) and when he often healed (the Sabbath), also sent a message. As John Drane writes in Son of Man,

It is striking that the kind of people Jesus healed—the deaf, dumb, and lame—do not feature at all in contemporary stories of Jewish healers. But these were the very things singled out as signs of the coming kingdom in an Old Testament passage that was widely regarded as messianic [Isaiah 35:5–6]. The coincidence would not be lost on those who were suspicious of Jesus' intentions. Nor would it escape their attention that the circumstances in which he cured people often infringed on Jewish laws.

Jesus restores sight to a blind man in this painting. Jesus performed such healings to show that he had been sent by God.

Galilee 57

Miracles

The emphasis on teaching in the Gospels underscores how important it was to Jesus. His mission, which he understood had been given to him by God, was to proclaim to the world God's message of the kingdom of God. Jesus probably saw himself as a teacher, not a prophet, and he employed the classic teaching method of his day. As New Testament scholar Rudolf Bultmann writes,

> As such [a teacher] he gathers around him a circle of pupils. As such he disputes over questions of the Law with pupils and opponents or with people seeking knowledge who turn to him.... This list could be easily continued; and indeed such examples must be kept in mind in order to understand how Jesus taught as a Jewish rabbi.[28]

Teaching, however, was only part of Jesus's mission. Equally important was his assertion that he, himself, was a herald of the kingdom of God. To show the world that this was so, that God had given him such power and authority, his ministry was filled with events considered to be miracles.

Miracles were much more readily accepted in Jesus's time than they are today. Most ancient cultures believed to some extent in the supernatural and held open the possibility that departures from

A Scientist's View

Dr. H. Tracy Hall, one of the twentieth century's premier chemists and the man who developed the first artificial diamond, writes that, much as he might wish as a scientist to understand Jesus's miracles, some things are beyond understanding, at least for now. He expresses this view in the article "A Scientist Looks at the Miracles of Jesus," found at www.htracyhall.org/pdf/miracles.pdf:

It would be audacious for a scientist to attempt to explain the miracles of Jesus. The "how," the "mechanism," or the "working details" by which they were accomplished are simply unknown to us. A miracle is an event that cannot be explained by principles currently understood by man.... Let there be no misunderstanding—as a scientist with an inquiring mind I would very much like to know the detailed principles by which Jesus' miracles were performed. I assume that by living His Gospel according to His laws, the day will come when it will be possible to know them. However, I must emphasize that our Father in heaven has made available to us the fruits of principles known to Him, without our having to possess His knowledge. They are made available by a simple key called faith.

the norm could be caused by gods, spirits, or even by people. Some individuals, it was widely believed, had access to special powers that enabled them to alter the natural course of events. As theologian J.D. Spiceland writes,

> Unlike the modern world, the ancient world was not suspicious of miracles. They were regarded as a normal, if somewhat extraordinary, part of life. Ancient people typically believed not only that supernatural powers existed, but also that they intervened in human affairs. Miracles, then, did not present a problem to the early Christians as they attempted to explain and relate their faith to the culture around them.[29]

Individuals who could perform miracles were thought to be either sorcerers or what the Greeks called *theios aner*, or "holy men." Sorcerers supposedly attained their magical powers through knowledge of the power that governed natural law, including the knowledge of how to alter it. Holy men, on the other hand, derived their power from a divine source and acted as a kind of conduit for the power of God or gods. Their prayers or entreaties, it was thought, were somehow more readily answered than those of ordinary people as if they had God's particular attention.

Jesus would have been in the latter category. He never claimed that miraculous powers originated in him, but told people to "understand that the Father is in me and I am in the Father" (John 10:38). His purpose seems to have been to demonstrate that he had been sent by God so that people would believe that his message was also divinely inspired.

Convincing The Disciples

Those people to be convinced included even his closest disciples. Jesus's first miracle, as related by the Gospels, was the changing of water into wine. By doing so, writes John, "He thus revealed his glory, and his disciples put their faith in him" (2:11).

That faith, however, was sometimes less than complete, much to Jesus's dismay. As Canadian theology professor Pierre Gilbert writes, "They [the disciples] just don't get it. They don't get him. And at times Jesus gets quite annoyed with them."[30] On one occasion, a man complained to Jesus that he had brought his son to the disciples to be healed, and they had failed. Jesus responded by calling the disciples "faithless and perverse" (Matthew 17:17). He told the man to bring the child directly to him, and one can almost hear him saying under his breath, "Must I do everything myself?"

Peter, the disciple upon whom Jesus most depended, was also the one who seemed to cause Jesus the most frustration. Bold and impetuous, Peter was quick to proclaim his faith, only to falter at a critical moment. Matthew tells that Jesus once, after preaching, told his disciples to get into their boat and that he would join them later after praying. When Jesus reached the shore, however, the boat was already offshore and unable to return because of an adverse wind. Realizing the boat could not come to him, Jesus walked out on the water toward the boat. The disciples were terrified, thinking he was a ghost, but Peter cried out, "Lord, if it's you, tell me to come to you on the water" (14:28). Jesus beckoned him and Peter began walking on the water, only to lose courage and begin to sink. Jesus reached out, saved him, and said, "You of little faith, why did you doubt?" (14:31).

Jesus as a Healer

Faith, indeed, seems to have been the primary point Jesus wanted to make—that God would take care of those who had faith in him and that faith was the key to putting divine power to work. In separate Gospel accounts, Jesus healed a blind beggar and a woman with a bleeding disorder whose belief in his power was so strong she thought she could be healed merely by touching Jesus's robe. In both cases, Jesus told them that it was their own faith that made them well.

News of Jesus's healings soon spread throughout the countryside. When he cured a man of leprosy by touching him, he cautioned the man, who was to show himself to priests as required by Jewish law, not to say how he had been cleansed. Instead, the man "went out and began to talk freely, spreading the news. As a result, Jesus could no longer enter a town openly but stayed outside in lonely places. Yet the people still came to him from everywhere" (Mark 1:45).

Not everyone, however, was willing to believe that Jesus had been sent by God. When the residents of four Galilean towns refused to acknowledge Jesus's power, despite having witnessed healings, he upbraided them, saying that such signs

Jesus rescues Peter after the disciple sinks while trying to walk on water. Jesus later chastised Peter for his lack of faith.

The Exorcisms

Since what now is known to be mental illness was widely ascribed to demonic possession in Jesus's day, it is no wonder that many people thought that he was just one more miracle worker. "Over a long period of time there had developed a class of exorcists to whom people turned in order to expel evil spirits and restore a sufferer's peace of mind," J.R. Porter writes in *Jesus Christ: The Jesus of History, the Christ of Faith*.

Jesus's opponents did not deny that he could perform exorcisms, but they denied that his power came from God. Instead, the Pharisees claimed, he expelled demons by the power of Beelzebub, or Satan, the prince of demons. Jesus neatly refuted the accusation, asking the Pharisees why a demon would cast out a demon.

In the Gospels, Jesus specifically gave his disciples authority to exorcise demons in his name. Indeed, Matthew and Luke tell of one man who was not even one of Jesus's followers doing so. Taking its cue from the Gospels, Christianity has retained exorcism as one of its rites, even though it is seldom used today.

would have been accepted elsewhere, even in the gentile cities of Tyre and Sidon.

Jesus also had little patience for those who would neither believe nor disbelieve, but who kept asking for more "signs." He asked them why, even though they could tell by looking at the sky if a storm was brewing, they were unable to recognize him for what he claimed to be. "Why does this generation seek a sign?" he said in Mark 8:12. "Truly, I say to you, no sign shall be given to this generation."

Jesus thus seems to have intended his miracles to be much more than demonstrations of power. They were direct challenges to the beliefs of those who witnessed them. Confronted with events so extraordinary, people were forced to choose. Was Jesus a messenger sent directly from God or not? "Once people witness Jesus' 'miracles,' they cannot avoid the question," writes Barry Smith, "but what they can avoid is the answer that Jesus' ability comes from God."[31]

Raising the Dead and Casting Out Demons

Easily the most spectacular of Jesus's reported miracles was the restoration of life to those who had died. The best-known instance is that of Lazarus, who, with his sisters Mary and Martha, was a good friend of Jesus. Jesus intended the raising of Lazarus to be a powerful sign to those who witnessed it. Just before calling

Galilee **61**

Lazarus forth from his tomb, he thanked God for his power, saying that he had performed the miracle "for the benefit of the people standing here, that they may believe that you sent me" (John 11:42).

In much the same way Jesus sought to demonstrate God's power over evil by performing exorcisms, the casting out of demons. He very likely shared the Jewish belief of the time that supernatural spirits had the power to intervene in people's lives either for good, in the case of angels, or evil, in the case of demons. When he commanded these demons to depart from people whose bodies they had taken over, his purpose was probably not only to heal the people, but also to demonstrate that his power—and God's—were stronger than the power of Satan, supposed ruler of evil spirits. J.R. Porter writes,

> For the synoptic Gospels, Jesus's authority over demons is closely associated with his authority as a teacher in that his healings and exorcisms confirmed the truth and power of his preaching. To the jealousy of his opponents, Jesus possessed authority over demons because he was recognized by the people at large as a charismatic prophet who—like the prophets in the Hebrew Scriptures—was directly inspired by the spirit of God.[32]

In the light of modern knowledge about mental illness, many of the exorcisms would have to be classified as healings. Likewise, some of the infirmities Jesus healed, such as paralysis, might have been more mental than physical. Others, however, were clearly miraculous in nature, such as the curing of blindness or the restoration of the dead.

Confronting Authority

Jesus's miracles, however, were a challenge not only to those who witnessed them, but also to the religious authorities of the day. As he traveled through Palestine, these authorities became ever more aware of him. They repeatedly challenged his views on the Law and how to obey it, but he adroitly turned their own arguments against them, teaching that God's law is higher than that of men.

Jesus was at his best when confronted by those who sought to trap him into making statements at odds with the Law. John tells that a group of Pharisees hauled before him a woman accused of adultery. Moses's Law, they reminded him, called for the woman to be stoned to death. What, they asked, was Jesus's view?

Jesus had been seated on the ground, teaching a lesson. When he heard the Pharisees, he stood, looked at them, and said, "Let him who is without sin among you be the first to throw a stone at her" (8:7). As Jesus resumed his lesson, the Pharisees looked at each other dumbstruck and, one by one, stole silently away.

Pharisees criticize Jesus for associating with a woman convicted of adultery in this Italian painting. Jesus associated with sinners to show God's love for all people.

Finally, Jesus looked up at the woman, asking where those who condemned her were. She replied that they had all departed. Jesus said, "Neither do I condemn you; go, and do not sin again" (8:11).

Religious and civil law were actually one and the same for Jews. The Law governed not only religious practices, but also every facet of everyday life, prescribing everything from diet to divorce. There was disagreement, however, on exactly what constituted the Law.

The Pharisees

The two primary religious groups were the Sadducees and the Pharisees. The Sadducees, comprising mostly the priests, held that the only valid Law was that given by God to Moses and contained in the Torah. The Pharisees, laymen who prided themselves on strict obedience to the Law, thought that the Law was open to expansion and interpretation and that they were the ones who should do the interpreting.

Galilee

The Pharisees

> *Readers of the Gospels might be forgiven for considering the Pharisees the villains of the story of Jesus of Nazareth. They constantly questioned him, trying to discredit him, and he just as constantly rebuked them as a "brood of vipers" (Matthew 12:34). Actually, as John Drane writes in* Son of Man, *a biased impression may have been given by early Christians, who viewed Pharisaic Judaism as far removed from Jesus's message and whose communities were in conflict with Jews:*
>
> It is not hard to understand the historical and sociological reasons for such antagonism. But theologically, things were not that simple. Most Jewish believers had a strong personal trust in God, and tried to keep the Old Testament Law as part of their faith response to what God had done for the life of their nation. They were not legalists, trying to blackmail God by their own moral goodness. On the contrary, they were honest and straightforward people and intensely devout.

Jesus's view was closer to that of the Pharisees than the Sadducees, but it was the Pharisees with whom he had the most contact—at least until his final days in Jerusalem. The Pharisees had the most influence among the common people, and consequently, as Porter writes, "the Pharisees no doubt saw Jesus as a threat to their religious authority and teaching. In their eyes, he was a provincial [inexperienced country boy] with no background of religious training, and they inevitably questioned whether his teaching, so different from scribal learning, could possess the authority of their own."[33]

Jesus's view, opposite that of the Pharisees, was that only God could make the Law. It might be studied and interpreted, but not added to. He often condemned religious authorities for caring more about strict observation of the Law than for what was at the base of the Law—honoring and worshipping God. On one occasion, when rebuked for not washing his hands before a meal, he said, "Now then, you Pharisees clean the outside of the cup and dish, but inside you are full of greed and wickedness," adding that while they observe the Law, they "neglect justice and the love of God" (Luke 11:39–42).

The Core of Jesus's Teaching

Jesus rejected the Pharisees' view that all aspects of the Law were equally important. His teachings indicate that he considered there to be a core around which much of the Law was constructed. For him, this core was grounded in a person's faith, belief, and spirit of good will. His view was incorporated in

Matthew 22:37–40. Asked by a Pharisee which of God's commandments was the greatest, he answered, "You shall love the Lord your God with all your heart, and with all your soul, and with all your mind. This is the great and first commandment. And a second is like it, You shall love your neighbor as yourself. On these two commandments depend all the law and the prophets."

This statement, in itself, was not controversial. The Essene community and other Jewish religious scholars emphasized love of God and love of mankind as the keys to righteousness. Where Jesus departed from the Pharisees and Sadducees was in his additional comment that the two commandments are more important than all burnt offerings and sacrifices (Mark 12:33). This was heresy to the Sadducees, whose livelihood as priests depended on offerings and sacrifices at the Temple in Jerusalem, and especially to the Pharisees, who prided themselves on punctilious obedience to all facets of the Law.

Jesus often directed his message to sinners, telling them that they should seek forgiveness from God.

One way Jesus showed his contempt for the Pharisees was to associate with people completely on the opposite end of the social scale—prostitutes, tax collectors, and other sinners. While he probably shared the Pharisees' belief that the righteous would be given eternal life by God and that sinners could attain righteousness by both repenting and changing their behavior, he differed in that he actively approached sinners instead of avoiding them and waiting for them to come to terms with God on their own.

Jesus's seeking out of sinners would have great significance for the future of Christianity. He was later to pass on this sense of urgency, of the nearness of God's kingdom, to his disciples and, ultimately, to all practitioners of Christianity. His message, passed through the disciples to future generations of Christians, was evangelism, from the Greek word for "good news." It is not enough, he seemed to be saying, to be secure in one's own piety, like the Pharisees; one must actively seek out others to show them the way to God.

Was one permitted, then, to break the Law—at least as the Pharisees saw it—and if so, in what circumstances? The part of the Law that Jesus was most often accused of breaking was the requirement to do no work on the Sabbath. Jesus responded by saying, "The Sabbath was made for man, not man for the Sabbath" (Mark 2:27). In other words, the Sabbath had been ordained by God as one of the Ten Commandments to Moses in order to provide people with a day of rest, dedicated to God, not to cause them hardship.

The Son of Man

All who encountered Jesus—believers, doubters, disciples, enemies—were ultimately confronted by the same central question. Who or what was this man from Nazareth? Jesus seldom answered the question directly. Instead, through his words and deeds, he challenged others to answer it for themselves: Was he the promised Messiah, the son of God, sent to redeem sinners and usher in God's kingdom?

While Jesus was notably reluctant to press such a claim, he seemed to be comfortable with other titles accorded him. He clearly referred to himself when he said that a prophet is not without honor, except in his own country, and in Luke he compared himself with the great Old Testament prophets Elijah and Elisha. Similarly, he accepted the titles of rabbi, master, and lord. "Master" and "lord," however, did not appear to have any special religious significance, but denoted a figure of authority.

Frequently, however, Jesus employed another term whose meaning has been the subject of much debate—"son of man." The phrase occurs eighty-two times in the Gospels and was clearly Jesus's preferred way of referring to himself. What did it mean? Everything or nothing, depending on the interpretation.

The phrase is found in the Old Testament book of Daniel, which says that

The Messianic Expectation

For most of his ministry, Jesus refrained from claiming to be the Messiah promised by Jewish prophets in the Old Testament, preferring to let his actions speak for him. This left many people wondering if he was the Messiah or, if not, exactly what he was, as John Drane writes in Son of Man:

When people looked at Jesus, they naturally compared him with their own picture of what the Messiah would be like when he came. With so many diverse views current, it is not surprising that there were many opinions as to whether Jesus could be the one. He certainly had the popular charismatic appeal that could be expected of the Messiah, and people of all sorts found themselves drawn to him. But he seemed either unwilling or unable to do many of the things popularly associated with the Messiah—like fighting the Romans, and re-establishing a Jewish state. And yet he talked about God's Kingdom having come, and of himself as a leading actor in the drama. No wonder that many people simply did not know what to make of him.

"there came one like a son of man. . . . And to him was given dominion and glory and kingdom, that all peoples, nations, and languages should serve him" (7:13–14). It is very likely, scholars say, that the phrase came to be identified with the promised Jewish Messiah.

Jesus sometimes seemed to use "son of man" in the messianic context, but some experts think the phrase may have had just the opposite meaning, that instead of signifying authority and power, it was a sign of humility. As Porter writes, "The Aramaic [the language spoken by Jews of Jesus's time] evidence suggests that a speaker might say 'the son of man' instead of 'I' out of modesty or reserve, and this could well be the case with Jesus, who often appears to have been cautious about making claims for himself."[34]

A third possibility is that Jesus used "son of man" as a term of humility in a different sense than mere modesty. One of the basic tenets of Christianity is that Jesus was both God and human and that he derived his humanity from Mary, his mother. If Jesus was aware of this dual nature, he might have used "son of man" in reference to his human side, not as a reference to his role as divine Messiah.

The Son of God

If Jesus was ambiguous in referring to himself as the "son of man," he was doubly careful about any claim, whether by himself

Jesus speaks to a Samaritan woman beside a well in this Spanish painting. The incident is one of the few in the Bible in which Jesus said he was the Jewish messiah.

or others, that he was the Messiah. Had he openly proclaimed himself to be the long-sought deliverer, the Jews would have misunderstood the nature of the delivery and would have looked to him to lead an armed uprising against Rome. And the Romans, while they might not have believed that the God of the Jews would raise up a mighty warrior to challenge their legions, were nevertheless watchful for, and ready to quash ruthlessly, any rebellion led by someone claiming to be the Messiah. As Rudolf Augstein writes, "if any man declared that he was the Messiah, he would have been expected to bring about an immediate end to Roman domination."[35]

Therefore, while the word *Messiah* and its Greek counterpart, *Christ*, appear often in the Gospels, it is never Jesus himself who utters them. In fact, he openly acknowledged himself to be the Messiah on only two occasions—once in a private conversation and again at his eventual trial.

The conversation occurred when Jesus accepted a drink of water from a Samaritan woman, much to her surprise, since Jews normally avoided any interaction with the Samaritans, a Palestinian sect that had broken away from mainstream Judaism. He spoke to her about the kingdom of God, and she said she knew that a Messiah was coming who would reveal all things. Jesus replied, "I who speak to you am he" (John 4:26).

Nevertheless, Jesus never said in so many words that he was the son of God, although others did. One of the best-known instances occurred when he asked the disciples who the people said that he was. They replied that he was considered a great prophet—another John the Baptist, Elijah, or Jeremiah. Then, perhaps to see if the disciples had truly understood what he had been teaching them, he asked, "But who do you say that I am?" Peter answered, "You are the Christ, the Son of the living God." As usual, Jesus did not specifically acknowledge the truth of what Peter said, but said only that this knowledge had been revealed to him by "my Father who is in heaven" (Matthew 16:15–17).

However cautious or guarded Jesus was in defining the role he believed God had given him, he was bound to achieve notoriety and thus increase the authorities' awareness of him. As Jesus grew more confident of the mission he felt God had given him, and as the people grew more confident of his powers, these authorities grew more uncomfortable. This Galilean carpenter with his parables and healings was now more than a nuisance. He was a threat, and threats must be eliminated.

Chapter 5

Jerusalem

No part of Jesus's life is as thoroughly described as its final week. Unlike accounts of his earlier life, the Passion Narrative—from the Latin *passio* or "suffering"—is rich in detail, almost an hour-by-hour chronology. These events must have made a vivid impression on those who handed the story down through the years.

From the very start of his ministry, Jesus seemed to be following some sort of timetable. Since the time he began preaching and performing miracles, his pronouncements and actions grew steadily bolder, more challenging to established authority. He seemed to know, or at least suspect, that a confrontation was at hand and may have deliberately led his disciples to Jerusalem in about A.D. 30 at the time of the Jewish feast of the Passover.

Many Christians assert that Jesus knew that he would be put to death and that it was part of his view of God's plan for him. The notion that he would be sacrificed in order to bring salvation to humanity had its roots in the Old Testament. The chief example comes from Isaiah, who writes that the savior would be "despised and rejected by men . . . we esteemed him not. Surely he has borne our griefs and carried our sorrows. . . . and the Lord has laid on him the iniquity of us all.. . . By oppression and judgment he was taken away" (53:3–8). In other words, God would raise up an individual who would take on himself the sins of all Israel—all humanity, Christians believe—and through his death reconcile the people with God.

This is the Gospels' position, but the authors were writing both from a theological point of view and with the benefit of hindsight. It is not at all certain what Jesus —much less his disciples—expected in Jerusalem. Perhaps, after all, God would take the opportunity to establish his kingdom on earth.

The Bible claims that at his death Jesus took on himself the sins of all humanity.

Clearly, some events of the Passion might have been invented or embellished later by the Gospel authors to project then-current theology onto the scene. "For them," writes Boers, "the reported events had symbolic significance. Their purpose was to bring out that significance, to which the question of historical accuracy was subservient."[36] It seems safe to say, despite a lack of incontrovertible evidence, that Jesus was executed. Many of the Gospel details, however, should be considered, in Crossan's words, "not history remembered but prophecy historicized."[37]

The Entry into Jerusalem

Jesus's entry into Jerusalem is an excellent example. The Old Testament prophet Zechariah had written, "Rejoice greatly, O daughter of Zion! Shout aloud, O daughter of Jerusalem! Lo, your king comes to you; triumphant and victorious is he, humble and riding on an ass, on a colt the foal of an ass" (9:9). Accordingly, the Gospels relate, Jesus paused on the outskirts of Jerusalem and told the disciples to go to a certain house where they would find, depending on the Gospel, either an ass with her colt or the colt alone. They obeyed, and Jesus rode the colt into the city.

The entry into Jerusalem took place only a few days after Jesus had reportedly raised Lazarus from the dead in Bethany, only a few miles away. Consequently, his fame was at its peak, and a multitude of people lined the road to get a glimpse of this Galilean of whom they had heard so much. Many were probably only curious, but others were ready

This version of Jesus's entry into Jerusalem is by an Italian artist. Those awaiting him wave palm branches, and the event has been memorialized by Christians as Palm Sunday.

The Sadducees

Although it was the Pharisees who constantly harassed Jesus throughout his ministry, it was another group—the Sadducees—who ultimately brought him to the trial leading to his death. Few in number but nevertheless extremely influential, they made up the ruling Jewish council known as the Sanhedrin, which handed Jesus over to the Romans.

The Sadducees' origins are unclear, but by Jesus's time they dominated the Jewish religious hierarchy. They were extremely conservative, rejecting everything but the Law as set forth in the Torah and thus did not accept the more recent views on life after death held by the Pharisees.

The Sadducees seem to have lacked the zeal of most of their countrymen, perhaps believing in, but not actually yearning for, the promised Messiah. Their goal seems to have been for Judaism to be preserved intact to whatever extent possible, and thus they were sometimes willing to cooperate with the Romans in civil matters.

---

to welcome Jesus as the Messiah. They spread their cloaks before him, waved palm branches, and shouted, "Hosanna to the Son of David! Blessed is he who comes in the name of the Lord! Hosanna in the highest!" (Matthew 21:9). The event is memorialized in Christianity as Palm Sunday.

Such a scene was bound to make Jewish leaders even more nervous than usual. Passover was always a time of great tension in Jerusalem. The city overflowed with pilgrims, and religious zeal was at its height. Each year there was talk of the Messiah and of throwing off the Roman yoke.

The Jewish leaders—the Pharisees and the chief priests at the Temple—had already made up their minds to get rid of Jesus after hearing about his raising of Lazarus. Their concept of the Messiah was probably the one shared by most Jews, and they feared that this upstart rural preacher would start a rebellion that would be brutally crushed by the Romans. The high priest Caiaphas argued that, to prevent such a bloodbath, "It is expedient for you that one man should die for the people, and that the whole nation should not perish" (John 11:50).

Therefore, the Sanhedrin—Judaism's ruling body—ordered that any who knew his whereabouts should report it so that he could be arrested. While Jesus's entry into the city was probably reported to the Temple authorities, they were unlikely to try to arrest him in such a public setting, fearing the crowd would come to his rescue.

Jesus drives the money changers from the Temple in this Belgian painting.

Driving the Money Changers from the Temple

Jesus was soon to give the Sanhedrin even more cause for alarm. Immediately after entering Jerusalem—or early the next morning in another version—he went to the great Temple, focal point of the Jewish religion.

The Temple in Jesus's time was the second, the original built by King Solomon having been destroyed by the Babylonians in 586 B.C. The new Temple had been constructed by Herod the Great over forty-six years and at great cost, largely to the Jewish taxpayers. To it, especially at Passover, came Jews from all parts of the Roman world. In the outer courtyard, merchants sold animals—pigeons and lambs—to be sacrificed. Since foreign money was "unclean," Jews from other countries had to exchange their Greek drachmas or Roman denarii for Jewish coinage.

Jesus, according to John's gospel, had been to the Temple at least once before, teaching there during the Feast of Tabernacles in the fall. Like all righteous Jews who were able, he may also have gone there at previous Passovers and should have known about the money changers and sellers of animals. It is difficult to explain, then, the event that took place. Enraged by what he saw as a desecration of worship, he seized a whip and expelled the merchants, overturning their tables and shouting, quoting the prophet Jeremiah, that they had made the temple a "den of robbers" (7:11).

What caused this sudden outburst of violence in one who preached peace? Some see the act as symbolic of a future time, as A.N. Wilson writes, "when God would overturn the present order and raise up Jesus."[38] However, a more pragmatic theologian, John Dominic Crossan, surmises that Jesus, who preached equality, "exploded in indignation"[39] at the Temple as the seat of those who oppressed the people.

Jesus, in fact, was no admirer of the pomp and wealth of the Temple and had recently predicted its destruction. In Luke 21 he preached that not one stone would be left atop another and that armies would surround Jerusalem. As it subsequently happened, the Temple was destroyed in A.D. 70 by Roman legions, and many scholars think that the author of Luke put the prophecy in Jesus's mouth after the event.

Much more enigmatic was Jesus's statement in John 2:19: "Destroy this temple and in three days I will raise it up." This has been widely interpreted as a prediction by Jesus—perhaps written after the fact by Mark—that he would be killed and, in three days, rise from the dead. Although Mark writes that the people did not understand what Jesus said, his predictions about returning from the dead seem to have been known by the priests.

At any rate, the Temple was where the pilgrims from around the world gathered, and it was there that Jesus preached his message over the next two days and, according to Matthew, healed "the blind and the lame" (21:14). The more people gathered to hear him, the more the high priests wanted to arrest him, but they dared not do so publicly. Each evening, apparently unnoticed and not followed, he left Jerusalem and returned to Bethany, where he was staying with Mary, Martha, and Lazarus.

Judas Iscariot

The priests needed someone close to Jesus who would betray him at some time when he could be arrested without risking a riot. They found their man in Judas Iscariot, one of Jesus's twelve closest disciples.

Judas Iscariot betrays Jesus with a kiss in this Byzantine mosaic. Some scholars think Judas was attempting to force Jesus to ignite a rebellion against Roman rule.

Judas Iscariot

Perhaps no other name in history is as closely linked with treachery than that of Judas Iscariot, the disciple of Jesus who, according to the Gospels, betrayed his master. Why he did so, however, remains a source of conjecture.

His name denotes that he came from the Palestinian city of Kerioth. He was the disciple in charge of purchasing supplies and seems to have been fond of money. Indeed, the Gospels suggest greed as the reason for Judas's betrayal, since the Temple authorities paid him thirty pieces of silver. However, writes Dr. Ralph Wilson in an article found at www.jesuswalk.com/lessons/21_37-22_6.htm, he may have had another reason:

One theory sees "Iscariot" as derived from Latin sicarius, which means "daggerman," a word applied to members of the Zealot movement. Thus Judas is a political zealot who believes that Jesus is the true Messiah who will free Palestine from Roman occupation. But he is disappointed that Jesus seems to be pursuing a spiritual and educational agenda rather than one which will lead to conflict with the Romans. Judas is convinced that if conflict with the Romans does occur, Jesus the Messiah will lead the nation to military victory. Thus the betrayal is a plot designed to force Jesus' hand into taking action against the Romans.

Two Gospels—Luke and John—say that Satan entered Judas's heart and prompted him to go to the high priest and offer to bring about Jesus's arrest. Matthew and Mark ascribe his motive to greed since he demanded payment. This seems unlikely since the sum agreed on—thirty pieces of silver—was not all that large, about the fine for injuring a man's horse. Some experts suggest that the story about payment was told in order to agree with an obscure passage in the Old Testament Book of Zechariah.

Judas's background is obscure. Some authorities claim his surname, Iscariot, denotes that he came from the Judean village of Kerioth. Others, however, say that the name is a distortion of the Latin word *sicarius*, or "dagger-man," a term applied to the members of the Zealot party that advocated armed rebellion. If the latter is true, it might provide a clue as to why Judas betrayed Jesus.

Jesus's preaching in the Temple had covered a wide range of subjects. Most of it dealt with love and peace and the kingdom of God—what it would be like, who could enter. But there were also passages that sounded as if some sort of cataclysmic events were imminent. Jesus said that "they will see the Son of man coming in clouds with great power and glory" (Mark 13:26). And he added, "This generation will not pass away before all these things take place" (13:30).

Some scholars think that Judas, on hearing this, thought that the great rebellion he sought was almost at hand. He may, then, have decided to incite that rebellion, handing Jesus over to his enemies in the hope he would prove to be the kind of Messiah that Judas wanted, calling down the forces of God on the Romans.

The Last Supper

Before the betrayal took place, however, another event occurred that would have enormous consequences for Christianity. Jesus gathered the twelve disciples together for an evening meal, traditionally held to have been eaten on a Thursday, that would eventually be known as the Lord's Supper or the Last Supper. While it is often assumed that this was the traditional Jewish Passover meal, this is by no means certain.

The Significance of the Last Supper

Whether or not the meal was the Passover feast, Jesus gave it great significance. He invited only the twelve disciples, excluding all others—even Mary, Martha, and Lazarus.

During the Last Supper, it is unlikely that Jesus and his disciples would have been seated at a table, as this painting shows.

From what the Gospels say, he obviously expected the meal to be the last he would eat with them, at least during his earthly life. He wanted the disciples to continue the ministry he had begun and told them so in several ways. He said to them, according to Luke, "I assign to you, as my Father assigned to me, a kingdom" (22:29).

John especially emphasizes the theme of discipleship. According to his Gospel, Jesus delivered a lengthy sermon in which he told the disciples, "I chose you and appointed you that you should go and bear fruit and that your fruit should abide" (15:16). Later, in a prayer to God, he said, "As thou didst send me into the world, so I have sent them into the world" (17:18). John's Gospel, however, is the least biographical and most theological of those in the New Testament. Many scholars therefore doubt that Jesus actually spoke such words, but think instead that the theme was expanded by the author as an inspiration to the early Christians who were trying to proclaim the new religion.

Much more likely to be accurate is the account of Jesus telling the disciples that one of them would betray him. The tradition of the betrayal by Judas and the similarity of the Gospel accounts make it likely that the event happened much as described. As the meal began, Jesus told the disciples, "Truly, I say to you, one of you will betray me, one who is eating with me" (Mark 14:18).

The disciples were thunderstruck and each began asking Jesus if he was the one. According to John, Jesus said, "It is he to whom I shall give this morsel [of bread] when I have dipped it" (13:26). He then gave the morsel to Judas and told him to go and do quickly what he had to do.

The other signal event of the Last Supper came when Jesus made the bread and wine on the table symbols of himself. Luke's version, which first appeared in one of Paul's letters, is the best known: "And he took bread, and when he had given thanks he broke it and gave it to them, saying, 'This is my body which is given for you. Do this in remembrance of me.' And likewise the cup after supper, saying, 'This cup which is poured out for you is the new covenant in my blood'" (22:19–20).

From this tradition arose the Christian ceremony of the Eucharist—from Greek for "thanksgiving"—to commemorate what Christians see as Jesus's sacrifice of himself to atone for the sins of humanity. It has remained the focal point of Christian worship ever since—in A.N. Wilson's words, "feeding the hearts and imaginations of men and women for two thousand years."[40]

The Mount of Olives

After the meal, Jesus led the disciples from the city to the nearby Mount of Olives to a garden called Gethsemane, or "olive press." He might well have been expecting trouble and may even have had some notion of flight or, perhaps, resistance. In Luke he told the disciples, before they left the meal, to take a purse or a bag and even to buy a sword if they did not have one. When the

The Agony in the Garden

Most scholars think that what passed through Jesus's mind in the Garden of Gethsemane on the night of his arrest remained private and could not have been known by the Gospel writers. However, to A.N. Wilson, writing in Jesus: A Life, *the Gospel account tells the story in Christian terms far more eloquently than a factual account:*

For the Christian believer and theologian, the Agony in the Garden is one of the most solemn moments in the Passion. It is the point where Christ in his human nature wishes that the cup of suffering could pass from him, but in his divine nature he knows that he, and he alone, can take upon himself the expiatory death which will deliver the world from sin. Such thoughts could not have passed through the mind of the historical Jesus, but an account of what actually went on in the Garden of Gethsemane would probably be unable to penetrate, as the Gospel accounts do, the very heart of suffering, so that every listener is caught up in the agony.... It is one of the most superb of all literary creations, outstripping the Iliad, and Aeschylus and Shakespeare at their most august and terrible.

This fourteenth-century painting shows Jesus praying in the Garden of Gethsemane while his disciples sleep nearby.

disciples answered that they had, among them, two swords, he answered, "It is enough" (22:38). Some experts say that Jesus used "sword" in a figurative sense, meaning the weapon of truth, and when the disciples once again missed his point, told them to drop the conversation.

Jesus, Luke wrote, often went to the Mount of Olives and might have known that Judas would lead the servants of the chief priests there to arrest him. Beforehand, however, he wanted to pray. He went off a short distance by himself, telling the disciples to keep watch. Instead, however, they fell asleep.

The Gospel accounts of Jesus's prayer—beseeching God to save him, if possible, from death—give a vivid picture of a man

Jerusalem 79

with doubts about his destiny and a very human fear of pain and suffering. Most scholars, however, share the view of A.N. Wilson, who writes, "By definition, since the Disciples are asleep, and Jesus would hardly have been able to write down an account of his evening in Gethsemane before being crucified the next day, his prayer in agony is a literary creation."[41] Also lending doubt to the story are the passages where Jesus predicts his death. If he, as a divine being, knew his fate, why would he seek to avoid it?

When his prayer, whatever it might have been, was finished, he aroused the sleeping disciples, chiding them for not having the willpower to keep watch as he had asked. Earlier in the evening, in fact, when Peter had boasted he would stay at Jesus's side no matter what happened, Jesus predicted, correctly, that Peter would deny he ever knew him. The story of Peter's denial has the ring of authenticity. He is thought to have lived until executed in Rome in A.D. 64, and it would have been entirely in character for him to confess his own weakness while preaching Jesus's message of forgiveness.

Quickly thereafter the peace of the garden was shattered by the arrival of the chief priests' servants, armed with swords and clubs and led by Judas. They had come to arrest Jesus. At first, the disciples resisted. One of them drew his sword and cut off an ear of one of the attackers. Jesus, however, wanted to avoid bloodshed. According to Matthew, he healed the wounded man and told the disciple to sheathe his sword, adding, "all who take the sword will perish by the sword" (26:52).

Judas, in order to identify the man whom the crowd was to seize, hailed Jesus as "Master" and kissed him on the cheek. Jesus went quietly. According to John, in fact, he said to the crowd, "I told you that I am he; so, if you seek me, let these men go" (18:8). Some writers have taken this passage to suggest that the betrayal by Judas may have even been prearranged by Jesus, who surrendered himself willingly in order to save his followers from arrest.

It was now probably very early on Friday morning. The premonitions that Jesus had felt coming to Jerusalem were about to become reality. Leaving the bewildered disciples behind, the priests' servants led Jesus away to his final confrontation with those officials determined to do away with him.

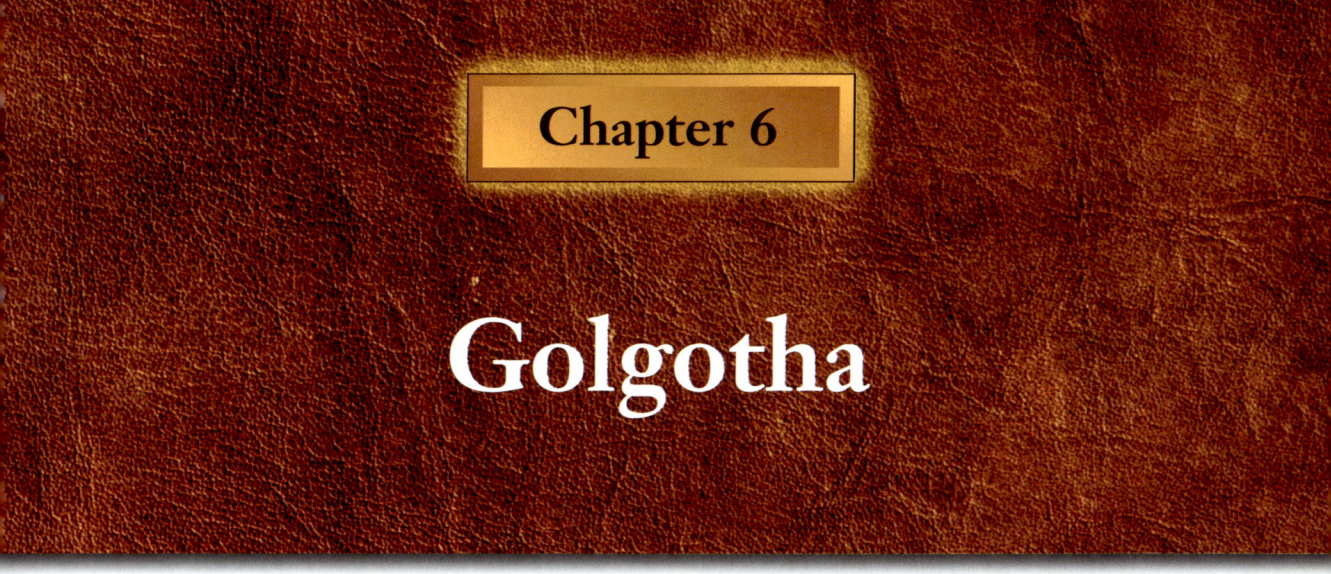

Chapter 6

Golgotha

Determined to rid themselves of Jesus of Nazareth and having brought about his arrest by betrayal and stealth, the Jewish authorities of Jerusalem were faced with a problem. What crime had he committed? On what legal basis could he be executed? Only after a few frantic hours, during which Jesus was shuttled back and forth among interrogators, could an excuse be found for condemning him to the most brutal and ignominious death the Roman legal system could devise—crucifixion.

Some scholars think that perhaps the Romans were, from the outset, part of the agreement to silence Jesus. John's Gospel includes soldiers among those who arrested Jesus at Gethsemane. If this is so, they had to be Roman soldiers. As J.R. Porter suggests, perhaps "the religious authorities only acted at the instigation of, and in collusion with, the Romans."[42] And Hendrikus Boers adds, "What evidently happened historically was a tradeoff—in order to prevent the danger of a threatened uprising, the Jewish authorities passed the responsibility for deciding Jesus' fate on to the Romans."[43]

Interrogation

Before being handed to the Romans, however, Jesus was taken to the house of the high priest, Caiaphas, to be questioned. Although often referred to as a trial, this was probably more of an interrogation. A trial would have been conducted at the Temple, not a private home, and not in the middle of the night. The Sanhedrin, or as many members as were present, were probably looking for some excuse, some legal grounds, that would allow them to hand him over to the Romans for execution.

To have claimed to be the Messiah, which Jesus had actually never done, a claim that threatened to usurp their authority, would not have been enough.

While the priests would have considered such a claim the act of a fanatic or, perhaps, a madman, it was not technically against Jewish law and certainly not punishable by death, a sentence only the Romans could carry out.

The Jewish authorities were under tremendous pressure. It was bad enough that their authority was threatened by this peasant from Galilee, but their real danger, as they probably perceived it, was that his followers would spark an insurrection, with disastrous results. Less than forty years earlier, for instance, Jewish leaders had been unable to prevent an uprising in the city of Sepphoris. The result was its destruction by the Romans and the mass crucifixion of its citizens.

It is unclear how much responsibility for Jesus's execution rests with the Jews and how much with the Romans. The Gospels seem to go out of their way to blame Jewish leaders, while portraying the Romans almost as innocent dupes. This distribution of blame, however, may be traceable to the time at which the Gospels

Jesus is brought before Caiaphas, the Jewish high priest, for questioning. Because this hearing occurred at night, it could not have been an official trial.

Romans and Priests

Although the high priests were the figures of greatest authority in Judaism, they were chosen, at least in Jesus's time, by the Romans. Realizing the volatility of the Jewish population, much of which looked for a Messiah to reestablish the Kingdom of Israel, the Romans were careful to appoint people who would cooperate with them in keeping order. Such a person, evidently, was Joseph Caiaphas, the man who, according to the Gospels, questioned Jesus of Nazareth and handed him over to the Romans as a revolutionary to be executed.

Caiaphas, whose father Annas had also been high priest, held the position from A.D. 18 to 36. He seems to have worked very closely with the Roman governor, Pontius Pilate, and historians have speculated on what lay behind his persecution of Jesus. Some think that Caiaphas feared that Jesus would stir up the people to such an extent as to cause a severe limitation on Jewish freedoms by the Romans; he thus was seeking the Jews' best interests. Other historians think that Caiaphas might have been bribed by Pilate to help keep the peace.

Caiaphas and Pilate were both removed from office in A.D. 36. What happened to Caiaphas then is unknown, but in 1990 an ossuary, or bone box, thought to contain his remains was discovered near Jerusalem.

---

were written, when the early Christians were both persecuted by the Jews and seeking to expand the new religion throughout the Roman world. As A.N. Wilson writes,

> The only hard historical fact which we possess is that Jesus was crucified: that is to say, he was condemned by the Romans, and this is a fact which the early Christian Church, themselves fearful of persecution from the Romans, did their best to obscure. They therefore blamed the death of Jesus on the Jews.[44]

Wilson further suggests that the Gospel details of Jesus's various interrogations are highly questionable, especially as there is no record of any of his followers being present during most of them. The exception is the first examination at the home of Caiaphas, the high priest, witnessed, the Gospels say, by Peter before his denial and perhaps by one other unnamed disciple.

The examination began with the questioning of witnesses against Jesus. Some reported having heard him say he would destroy the Temple in three days, but their testimony did not always agree. Finally, Caiaphas asked Jesus directly if he was the Messiah, the Gospels using the Greek

"Christ." Jesus answered either "I am" (Mark 14:62) or "You have said so" (Matthew 26:64). He then repeated what he had said earlier in the week while preaching in the Temple, that they "will see the Son of man seated at the right hand of Power, and coming with the clouds of heaven" (Mark 14:62).

At this, the high priest tore his robes in anger, accused Jesus of blasphemy, and asked those present for their judgment, which was that Jesus deserved death. The officials present did not sentence him to death, however, having no power to do so. First, such a sentence could be given only at an official trial and then only by the Romans. Second, claiming to be the Messiah was not a capital offense.

In speaking about coming in power, however, Jesus may have given Caiaphas an idea. If Jesus was claiming any kind of kingship, it could be construed as treason against Rome. It may have been this possibility that led the Jewish officials to the next step, taking Jesus before the Roman governor, Pontius Pilate.

Pontius Pilate

Pilate had been procurator, or governor, of Judea for about five years and had a reputation as a firm, if not ruthless, administrator. His headquarters were not in Jerusalem, but in the port city of Caesarea. It was logical, however, for him to have been in Jerusalem with a large body of troops at Passover in case of trouble.

The Jews must have realized that Pilate would have no interest in any religious controversy and that their best chance of having Jesus executed was on a charge of treason. They must have suggested such a charge immediately, for Pilate's first question to Jesus was "Are you the King of the Jews?" Just as he had replied to Caiaphas, Jesus answered, "You have said so" (Matthew 27:11).

The priests countered with several unspecified accusations. Perhaps they dealt only with religious matters instead of treason because Pilate said, "I find no crime in this man" (Luke 23:4). The priests were adamant.

Up to now, the questioning had been in a courtyard of the Roman praetorium, or palace, since the chief priests did not want to enter a place where foreign gods were worshipped. In John's Gospel, the scene then shifted to the inside, where Pilate summoned Jesus for a private conversation and asked him if he was, indeed, king of the Jews. Jesus replied, "My kingship is not of this world; if my kingship were of this world, my servants would fight, that I might not be handed over to the Jews" (18:36).

Jesus's reply is significant in both theological and historical terms. Theologically, it carried forward one of John's central themes—Jesus's kingship. From a historical perspective, the difficulty with the passage is how anyone recorded it, if the exchange really took place. If Jesus did say this to Pilate, however, it probably made Pilate even more sure of Jesus's innocence.

However, Pilate was in a quandary. He did not want to anger the priests, and he wanted to avoid a possibly violent protest, but he saw no reason to condemn Jesus. He began to look for a way out and, according to the Gospels, tried two.

First, Luke writes, Pilate seized on the priests' comment that Jesus was from Galilee. If he is a Galilean, Pilate reasoned, he fell under the authority of Herod Antipas, who happened to be in Jerusalem for the Passover. He promptly ordered Jesus to be taken to Antipas.

The Galilean ruler was, according to Luke, very curious about this man who had been creating such a stir in his country. He peppered Jesus with questions—what questions, the Gospel does not say—and entreated him to perform some miracle. Jesus stood silent, and Antipas at length gave up. He and his soldiers mocked their prisoner and sent him back to Pilate.

Barabbas

Although Pilate doubtless had hoped to have seen the last of Jesus, he now tried another method of ridding himself of this troublesome preacher. The Gospels say that it was Pilate's custom at Passover to allow the people to choose a prisoner to be released. He offered a crowd, evidently quickly assembled by the priests, a choice between Jesus and Barabbas, who, according to Mark, was in prison for murdering someone during an uprising. The crowd, at the instigation of the priests and probably much to

Pontius Pilate became governor of Judea in A.D. 26 and was recalled ten years later after he massacred a group of Samaritans.

Pilate's surprise and dismay, called for Barabbas. Pilate then asked the crowd what they wanted him to do with Jesus. Crucify him, the people shouted back.

The answer must have surprised Pilate. Crucifixion was the most severe punishment in Roman law, usually reserved for those who had committed the most serious crimes, such as treason. Its very brutality was supposed to be a deterrent to anyone who contemplated such a crime. Whatever Jesus might have done, Pilate did not think it merited crucifixion. "Why, what evil has he done?" he asked the crowd. "I have found in him no crime deserving death; I will therefore chastise [whip] him and release him" (Luke 23:22).

But the crowd, stirred to a frenzy by the priests, cried even louder for Jesus to be crucified. Pilate gave in. He ordered a basin

This Byzantine painting shows Pontius Pilate ceremonially washing his hands, thus denying blame for Jesus's death.

of water and washed his hands, symbolically clearing himself of any blame. According to Matthew, Pilate said, "I am innocent of this man's blood; see to it yourselves." The crowd answered, "His blood be on us and on our children" (27:24–25).

Many scholars consider the entire story of Barabbas, the shouting crowd, and Pilate's capitulation to be fiction, the most blatant example of the Gospel writers' objective of blaming the Jews for Jesus's execution. There is no record of Pilate or any Roman governor releasing a prisoner at Passover, much less letting the people choose which one. Giving in to an unruly mob, moreover, is counter to everything known about Pilate, about whom John Dominic Crossan writes, "Brutal crowd control was his specialty."[45]

The passage describing the crowd's willingness, not only to assume responsibility, but to pass it along to future generations is likewise difficult to explain away. As Spoto writes, "It does no good to attempt a softening of this motif."[46] What must be remembered, however, is that Matthew is thought to have been writing at a time when there was extreme bitterness between Judaism and the young Christian religion. Wilson writes that the Gospels "are intent on blaming the death of Jesus on the Jews. This is because Christianity started life as a Jewish heresy." Unfortunately, this passage has been the source of centuries of hatred and violence against Jews on the part of Christians. "Such a distortion of history would not have been so serious had it not been used as an excuse for two thousand years of Christian anti-Semitism,"[47] Wilson adds.

If Pilate had truly turned the entire matter over to the Jews, Jesus might have been taken out of the city and stoned to death, the traditional Jewish punishment for blasphemy, while the Romans conveniently looked the other way. The Gospels say, however, that Pilate instead turned Jesus over to his own troops for a Roman crucifixion.

The Flogging

Before the execution, however, Jesus was flogged. This was customary before crucifixion as reported by both the Jewish historian Josephus and the Roman historian Livy. The whip used was very much like the "cat-o'-nine-tails" later used aboard ships—a short-handled affair with multiple leather thongs. The thongs ended in lead tips into which might be imbedded bits of glass or bone intended to break the skin.

Flogging before crucifixion served two purposes. First, it was part of the punishment, meant to inflict pain. Also, however, it weakened the victim and lessened the time it took for him to die on the cross. Some condemned men, in fact, were inadvertently killed by the flogging before they could be crucified. If Pilate, indeed, thought Jesus innocent, he might have ordered a severe flogging in order to spare him greater agony later.

Jesus is mocked by Roman soldiers in this painting. Jesus was whipped, and a crown of thorns was pressed down on his head to mock his kingship.

Jesus's treatment by the soldiers is one of the few instances where Old Testament prophecy seems to have met historical fact. It is extremely likely, since he was crucified, that Jesus was also whipped. This would fulfill the messianic prophecies of Isaiah that "upon him was the chastisement that made us whole, and with his stripes we are healed" (53:5) and that "I gave my back to the smiters, and my cheeks to those who pulled out the beard; I hid not my face from shame and spitting" (50:6).

Via Dolorosa

More humiliation lay ahead. Crucifixion was intended to be as public a spectacle as possible. Therefore, the condemned man was forced to carry his cross to the place of execution—not the entire cross, as is often pictured, but the shorter, transverse beam. Accordingly, Jesus had the heavy wooden beam put on his already wounded shoulders, and he was marched out of Jerusalem along the street that today still bears the name Via Dolorosa, or "Way of Suffering."

After the flogging, the Roman soldiers mocked Jesus. If he was, indeed, a king, he ought to look like one. They placed a purple robe around his shoulders—shoulders probably shredded from the barbed whip—and pressed down on his head a crown made of thorns. They put a reed in his hand in mockery of a scepter, then beat him with it and spit upon him.

Tradition has it that Jesus fell three times on the way to the place of execution. The Gospels do not mention him falling in so many words, but it seems likely since an onlooker, Simon of Cyrene, was pressed into service to carry the cross.

According to Luke, a great crowd followed Jesus and his Roman escort. Since crucifixion was a public spectacle, such a procession probably took place. Luke used it to describe a scene in which Jesus turned toward a group of crying women, telling them, "Daughters of Jerusalem, do not weep for me, but weep for yourselves and for your children" (23:28). This passage, scholars think, is another reference to the destruction of the Temple by the Romans in A.D. 70.

At length, the group reached the hill known as Golgotha, or "place of the skull"—also known, from the Latin word for "skull," as Calvary. In addition to Jesus, two other men were to be crucified. They are described as either criminals or robbers in the Gospels, but they were more likely revolutionaries who had taken part in some uprising, perhaps the same one involving Barabbas.

The Crucifixion

Then, probably at about noon, the execution took place. Crucifixion, said to have been invented by the Persians, was used by the Romans as the most degrading form of capital punishment. The usual practice was to nail the victim's arms to a crosspiece, not through the hands, as so often pictured in Jesus's case, but through the wrists in order to support the body's weight. The

Nails at the Crucifixion

Many paintings or other representations of Jesus's crucifixion show him lashed by ropes to the cross instead of nailed, as related in the Gospels. Indeed, some scholars long contended that nails were never used because they could not have supported the weight of the body. Besides, the argument went, no evidence of the use of nails had ever been found.

Such evidence, however, made a dramatic appearance in 1968. Archaeologist Vassilios Tzaferis, who retired in 1999 as director of excavations and surveys for the Israel Antiquities Authority, discovered four tombs near Mt. Scopus, north of Jerusalem. In an ossuary in one of the tombs was the skeleton of a man identified as Yohanan Ben Ha'galgal. A large, 7-inch (17.5cm) spike had been driven through both heels.

Tzaferis concluded that the man had been crucified with both heels nailed to one side of the upright of a cross with a single spike. Further substantiating the Gospels' description of a crucifixion, both legs were broken. This would have been done to prevent the legs from supporting the body's weight, making it more difficult for the victim to breathe and thus hastening death.

legs sometimes were lashed to the upright post, but the feet might also be nailed through the heels.

Once placed in this position, the victim had to push up with the feet, lessening the strain on the arms in order to breathe. As the victim became weaker through loss of blood, this became increasingly difficult, leading finally to death by suffocation.

Although the crucified Jesus is commonly portrayed with nails driven through the palms, they were more likely through the wrists.

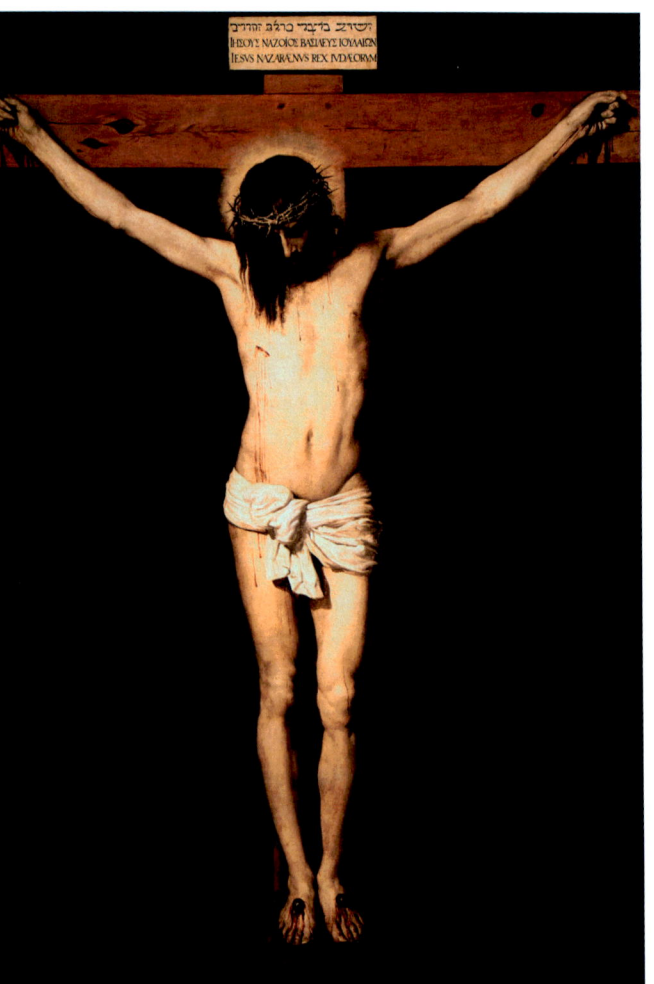

It was the Roman custom to place on the cross a sign stating the victim's crime. The sign ordered by Pilate read—in Latin, Greek, and Hebrew—"Jesus of Nazareth, the King of the Jews." While many have seen the sign as another way of mocking Jesus, Pilate might have had something else in mind. He might have been mocking the Jewish leaders, instead.

Certainly, the priests were upset with the sign. They urged that it be changed to read "This man said, 'I am king of the Jews.'" But Pilate had had enough of the priests and their demands. He told them, "What I have written, I have written" (John 19:22).

According to the Gospels, Jesus hung on the cross for about three hours. Witnessing his agony were several women, including his mother, who seems to have overcome her initial doubts and joined his movement. Other witnesses, the kind one would often see at public executions, mocked Jesus and told him, if he were really king of the Jews, to save himself.

Yet another Roman custom decreed that the clothing of executed criminals belonged to the executioners. Accordingly, as the three men hung in their agony, the soldiers gambled to see how to divide up the meager possessions. Thus yet another prophecy would be fulfilled: "They part my garments among them. And upon my vesture do they cast lots" (Psalm 22:18).

Jesus endured his pain and suffering, for the most part, in silence. At one point, however, it seemed as if his moment of human

The Shroud of Turin

After the crucifixion, according to the Gospels, Jesus's body was wrapped in a shroud and placed in a tomb donated by Joseph of Arimathea. When women came later to visit the tomb, they found no body, only the shroud left behind. Many people believe that the same shroud still exists in the Italian city of Turin.

The Shroud of Turin is a piece of linen 171 inches (434cm) long and 43 inches (109cm) wide. It exhibits what appears to be the image of the back and front of a man, as if the man were laid on one half of the cloth with the other folded over him. The image includes what some people think are bloodstains, and there are marks on the image consistent with the wounds that Jesus supposedly suffered.

The Shroud of Turin dates at least from 1357, when it was displayed in Lirey, France. It was moved to Turin in 1578 and has been exhibited publicly only very rarely, the last time in 1998. Because of the controversy over its authenticity, the Catholic Church agreed in 1998 to submit a small piece of the cloth to radiocarbon dating to determine its age.

Three different laboratories in three different countries came up with the same results—that the cloth was made sometime between A.D. 1260 and 1390. Despite the findings, many Christians insist that the shroud is the burial garment of Jesus.

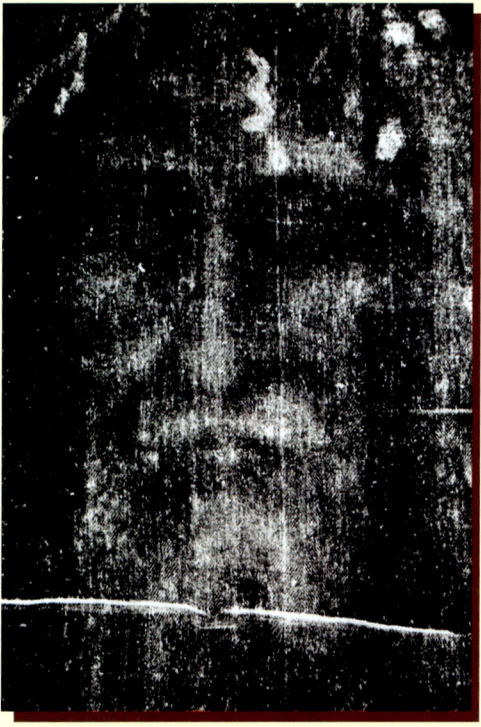

Many believe this image on the Shroud of Turin is the face of Jesus.

weakness in the garden of Gethsemane returned. According to Matthew (27:46) and Mark (15:34), Jesus cried out, "My God, my God, why hast thou forsaken me?" While these might seem to be words of despair, they are actually the opening words of Psalm 22, which goes on to promise deliverance: "For dominion belongs to the

Lord, and he rules over the nations. Yea, to him shall all the proud of the earth bow down" (28–29). As Cross writes, "It is credible, and indeed probable, that such a devout Jew as Jesus would, in his last agony, find comfort in reputing to himself the awesome words of this psalm, which go on from despair to triumph."[48]

Finally, at about three o'clock in the afternoon, Jesus cried out, "It is finished" (John 19:30) and died. Shortly afterward, the soldiers proceeded to break the legs of the two thieves in order to hasten their deaths. When they found Jesus already dead, they left his legs alone, but one soldier, probably to make sure he was dead, pierced his side with a spear, thus fulfilling a messianic prophecy by Zechariah.

The Tomb

Jewish custom decreed that, whenever possible, a person who died during the day should be buried by sundown. It was not clear, however, whether the Romans would allow Jesus to be buried at all. Part of the horror of crucifixion was that the body was left hanging on the cross to be picked apart by buzzards and crows. It was a part of the punishment since, according to many religions of the ancient world, the destruction of a body deprived the deceased of any chance at an afterlife.

However, Joseph of Arimathea, a member of the Sanhedrin who had not agreed with his colleagues about Jesus, asked Pilate to allow him to place Jesus's body in his own tomb. Pilate agreed, perhaps still disturbed at having acquiesced in the execution of a man he believed to be innocent.

Joseph and his friend Nicodemus had the body of Jesus removed, wrapped in a linen shroud, and placed in the tomb. According to Mark, there was not enough time before sundown and the start of the Jewish Sabbath to properly prepare it for burial with spices. That would have to be done later.

The priests still were not entirely satisfied. They remembered that Jesus had said that he would rise from the dead, and they feared that the disciples would steal the body and then proclaim he had done so. Probably the last thing Pilate wanted was for the controversy over Jesus to continue. He ordered that a heavy stone be rolled across the tomb entrance and that Roman soldiers guard the site.

Doubtless both the Temple authorities and the Romans thought that this was the end of the matter. The person considered a blasphemous rabble-rouser by the former and a potential rebel by the latter was dead and his followers in hiding. However, writes Crossan, "What could not have been predicted and might not have been expected was that the end was not the end."[49] The story of Jesus, as believed by Christians, was just beginning.

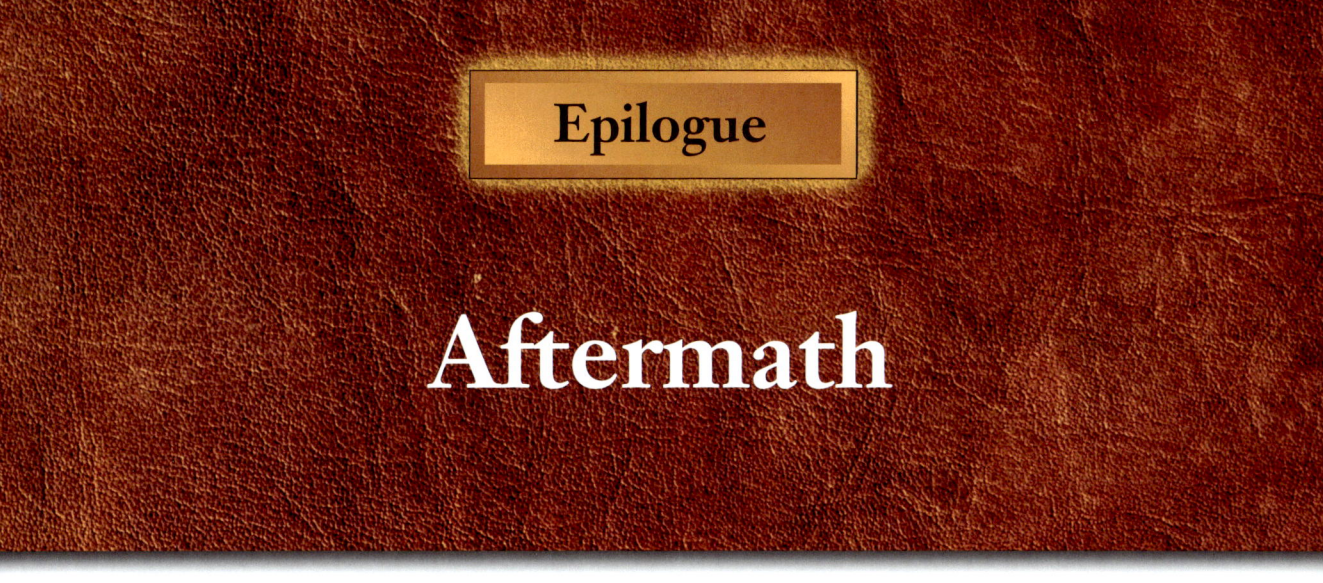

Epilogue

Aftermath

The greatest importance of Jesus of Nazareth lies not in his life but in what came after it. The movement he led might have been stillborn, dying with him on the cross, had not something else happened. The same disciples who had deserted him suddenly were willing to carry his message forward, risking torture and death in the process, and laying the groundwork for one of the world's great religions. Surely, writes Edwin Yamauchi, "something earth shaking must have transformed"[50] them. That something was their belief that Jesus had come back from the dead.

The Women at the Tomb

In turning from the life of Jesus to what Christians believe was his resurrection, one must depart from biography into the realm of belief. There were no witnesses, no Gospel accounts of how it may have taken place. Yet the resurrection, Spoto writes, "is not susceptible of historical proof or disproof. What can be shown, however, is what we might call the crater left by the explosion. We can see and assess the narratives about the faith of the apostles, who beheld him [Jesus] in some way that transformed their bafflement, fear, and hesitation."[51]

The Gospels disagree as to exactly what happened on Sunday—the day Christians would know hereafter as Easter. Someone went to the tomb. Matthew, Mark, and John say that at the least Mary Magdalene, a follower from whom Jesus had once exorcised seven demons, was there. She was accompanied in Matthew and Mark only by someone named Mary who possibly was Jesus's mother. Luke says that the tomb was visited by an indefinite number of women, one of whom might have been Jesus's mother. According to John, Mary Magdalene was alone.

This sixth-century mosaic shows a winged angel speaking to two women at Jesus's empty tomb. According to Mark's Gospel, the women were Mary Magdalene and another Mary, perhaps Jesus's mother.

The role of women in the story is significant. Many of those who question the authenticity of the resurrection have claimed that the disciples invented the entire episode. If this is so, defenders say, why would they have made women, very much second-class citizens in Jesus's time, the key witnesses? As English theologian C.F.D. Moule writes, "It is difficult to explain how a story . . . came to be framed in terms almost exclusively of women witnesses, who, as such, were notoriously invalid witnesses according to Jewish principles of evidence."[52]

Of the Gospel stories about what happened at the tomb, Matthew's is most dramatic. As the two Marys reached the site, there was a great earthquake and "an angel of the Lord descended from heaven and came and rolled back the stone, and sat upon it" (28:2). Calming the frightened women, he told them that Jesus was not there, that he had risen. He instructed the women to go tell the disciples of the miracle and that Jesus would go to Galilee, where the disciples would see him.

Matthew now includes an event found nowhere else. Guards, presumably those who had been at the tomb, told the Temple authorities what had happened, whereupon the guards were silenced with bribes and told to spread the story that the disciples had stolen the body. Then Matthew writes, "and this story has been spread among the Jews to this day" (28:15). Thus it seems clear that, at the time Matthew was writing, when there was deep division between Jews and Christians, the story of the stolen body was in vogue.

The Resurrection

One reason that the resurrection of Jesus was so difficult for Jews—then and now—to accept is that, while Jesus was thoroughly Jewish in his outlook, a return to life does not fit the messianic tradition. As recently as 1996, a council of Jewish rabbis passed a resolution that said, "There is not and has never been a place in Judaism for the belief that [the Messiah] will bring his Messianic mission only to experience death, burial and resurrection before completing it."[53]

The Jewish Pharisees, with whom Jesus had many beliefs in common, accepted the

Mary Magdalene

One of the most controversial questions in Christianity is whether Jesus had female disciples. Historically, most church authorities have held that, although he certainly had women followers, only men were disciples. This tradition has often been cited as a reason for denying women status as clergy.

Luke's Gospel, however, states that women accompanied Jesus and the twelve male disciples and supported his ministry with their own money. One such woman—and the one for whom the best case for discipleship can be made—was Mary Magdalene.

The New Testament says little about her—only that Jesus freed her of seven devils and that she was one of the women at the tomb after the crucifixion. The apocryphal Gospel of Peter (www.earlychristianwritings.com/text/gospel peter.html), however—thought to have been written about A.D. 150—specifically refers to Mary as "disciple."

Another ancient document written about the same time is the Gospel of Mary Magdalene (www.gnosis.org/library/marygosp.htm). In it, Peter says to Mary, "Sister, we know that the Savior loved you more than the rest of women. Tell us words of the Savior which you remember—which you know but we do not, nor have we heard them."

The Roman Catholic Church does not acknowledge either work. In fact, Pope Gregory I equated Mary to a prostitute in a sermon in 591, and the image of her as a sinful woman has endured. Only in the 1970s did the Church admit that such an image was not supported by the Bible.

The disciples raise their hands in amazement as the risen Jesus shows them the wounds in his hands resulting from the crucifixion.

idea of an afterlife, but one in which the dead would have a spiritual, not bodily, existence. The people whom Jesus had raised from the dead, such as Lazarus, seem to have been normal human beings afterward. The resurrected Jesus of the Gospels, however, was something in between. He had entered, Spoto writes, "a completely new form of existence, not restricted by time, place or death and, we may logically add, completely different from [any normal] organism of flesh and blood."[54]

In the Gospels' final scenes, Jesus—alive again—visited with the disciples. He was not a ghost or spirit, but a corporal being who ate and drank with them. He commissioned them to spread his message about the kingdom of God to all people in all lands. He then departed from them, saying they would not see him again until the final establishment of God's kingdom on earth, the so-called second coming.

The issue of the second coming of Jesus poses a contradiction. On one hand, Jesus had said, according to Luke, that men who lived in his time would see the Messiah come in power and glory. Such a second coming, at least in an apocalyptical sense, did not happen for Jesus's generation and still has not occurred. Critics such as Jewish scholar Pinchus Stolper say, then, that the "idea of a second coming is pure rationalization of Jesus' failure to function in any way as a Messiah. . . . The idea is purely a Christian invention."[55]

Was the entire resurrection an invention? The concept is so much beyond human understanding that the question continues to be asked. It is impossible to answer from a historical point of view. Wilson writes that with religions, it is often "impossible to say which came first—the cult or the story which explains the origin of the cult."[56]

Did Jesus rise from the dead? Indeed, did he ever live at all? Did he say any of the things attributed to him? Are the virgin birth, the star of Bethlehem, the healings and miracles all fables? The historical accuracy of the events of his life is almost irrelevant. What is important is that, from all historical accounts, his disciples firmly believed that Jesus was the Messiah, that he was resurrected from the dead, and that he would return.

The Importance of Jesus

The importance, then, of the life of Jesus of Nazareth is that his teachings and the belief of his followers in his—and ultimately their—resurrection provided the foundation on which the Christian religion was built. It may be, and in fact is probable, that Jesus, a devout Jew, had no intention of founding a worldwide movement that would bear his name, but that is nevertheless what happened.

And thus, in the name of this long-ago Jewish peasant, universities have been founded and hospitals established. Centuries of the world's greatest art and music have been devoted to his memory. His modern-day disciples have been inspired to minister to the sick, needy, friendless, and oppressed. Even our history is measured by the years before and since he lived.

To be sure, not everything done in Jesus's name has been in keeping with his message of peace and love. Christians have fought bloody wars against people of other faiths, attempting to spread with the sword what Jesus did with parables and healing. Christians have even slaughtered other Christians over what would probably seem to Jesus minor points of doctrine.

Some critics claim that there have been other people more important than Jesus. A.N. Wilson, for instance, ranks him in influence below the philosophers Plato and Aristotle, the mathematician Euclid, the founder of Islam Mohammed, the astronomer Copernicus, and the political theorist Karl Marx, among others. Yet given both the breadth and depth of Christianity's impact as the religion of the Western European culture that has dominated much of the world, it is difficult to imagine that any single person could have made a greater impression on history. As Susan Perlman, a Jew converted to Christianity, writes, "If Jesus had merely lived and died, the world would not have been forever altered by his coming. But his resurrection puts Jesus at the scene of every episode in history."[57]

Notes

Introduction: So Much from So Little

1. All quotations from the Bible are from the Revised Standard Version published by the University of Virginia Electronic Text Center. http://etext.lib.virginia.edu/rsv.browse.html.
2. Flavius Josephus, *Antiquities of the Jews*, Book 18. Translated by William Whiston. *The Works of Flavius Josephus.* www.ccel.org/j/josephus/works/ant18.htm.

Chapter 1: Bethlehem

3. Hendrikus Boers, *Who Was Jesus?* New York: Harper and Row, 1989, p. 20.
4. John Dominic Crossan, *Jesus: A Revolutionary Biography*. New York: HarperCollins, 1989, p. 18.
5. Malcolm Muggeridge, *Jesus: The Man Who Lives*. New York: Harper and Row, Publishers, 1975, p. 34.
6. Early Christian Writings, *The Protoevangelium of James*. Roberts-Donaldson English translation. Early Christian Writings. www.earlychristianwritings.com/text/infancyjamesroberts.html.
7. J.R. Porter, *Jesus Christ: The Jesus of History, the Christ of Faith*. New York: Oxford University Press, 1999, p. 69.
8. Crossan, *Jesus: A Revolutionary Biography*, p. 15.

Chapter 2: Nazareth

9. New Advent, *The Gospel of Pseudo-Matthew*, Chapter 26. *The Fathers of the Church*. www.newadvent.org/fathers/0848.htm.
10. Gnostic Society Library, *The Arabic Gospel of the Infancy of the Savior*, Chapter 38. www.gnosis.org/library/infarab.htm.
11. *The Gospel of Pseudo-Matthew*, Chapter 30.
12. *The Gospel of Pseudo-Matthew*, Chapter 31.
13. Quoted in David Bivin, "Jesus' Education." *Jerusalem Perspective Online*, www.jerusalemperspective.com/Default.aspx?tabid=27&ArticleID=1453.
14. Quoted in Bivin, "Jesus' Education."
15. *Arabic Gospel of the Infancy of the Savior*, Chapter 55.

Chapter 3: The Jordan

16. Quoted in James D. Tabor, "The Signs of the Messiah: 4Q521." *The Jewish Roman World of Jesus* (University of North Carolina - Charlotte Religious Studies Catalog). www.religiousstudies.uncc.edu/jdtabor/4q521.html.
17. Anthony M. Ludovici, *Man: An Indictment*. www.anthonymludovici.com/mi_11.htm.

18. Colin Cross, *Who Was Jesus?* New York: Atheneum, 1970, p. 59.
19. Barry D. Smith, *Life of Jesus*, Atlantic Baptist University, http://www.abu.nb.ca/Courses/NTIntro/LifeJ/BaptismJesus.htm.
20. Boers, *Who Was Jesus?*, p. 30.
21. Porter, *Jesus Christ: The Jesus of History, the Christ of Faith*, p. 83.
22. Muggeridge, *Jesus: The Man Who Lives*, p. 50.
23. Quoted in A.N. Wilson, *Jesus: A Life*. New York: W.W. Norton and Company, 1992, p. 109.
24. Josephus, *Antiquities of the Jews*, Book 18.
25. Pheme Perkins, *Jesus as Teacher*. Cambridge, England: Cambridge University Press, 1990, p. 29.

Chapter 4: Galilee

26. Crossan, *Jesus: A Revolutionary Biography*, p. 58.
27. Donald Spoto, *The Hidden Jesus*. New York: St. Martin's Press, 1998, p. 138.
28. Rudolf Bultmann, *Jesus and the World*. Translated by Louise Pettibone Smith and Erminie Huntress Lantero. New York: Charles Scribner's Sons, 1934, p. 99.
29. Quoted in BELIEVE Religious Information Source. www.mb-soft.com/believe/txo/miracle.htm.
30. Pierre Gilbert, "Moving Toward Greatness." *Radio Messages*, Canadian Mennonite University. www.cmu.ca/faculty/pgilbert/radio_messages/moving_toward_greatness.shtml.
31. Smith, *Life of Jesus*. www.abu.nb.ca/Courses/NTIntro/Life/HealerJesus.htm.
32. Porter, *Jesus Christ: The Jesus of History, the Christ of Faith*, p. 92.
33. Porter, *Jesus Christ: The Jesus of History, the Christ of Faith*, p. 103.
34. Porter, *Jesus Christ: The Jesus of History, the Christ of Faith*, p. 169.
35. Rudolf Augstein, *Jesus Son of Man*. Translated by Hugh Young. New York: Urizen Books, 1977, p. 61.

Chapter 5: Jerusalem

36. Boers, *Who Was Jesus?*, p. 66.
37. Crossan, *Jesus: A Revolutionary Biography*, p. 145.
38. Wilson, *Jesus: A Life*, p. 187.
39. Crossan, *Jesus: A Revolutionary Biography*, p. 133.
40. Wilson, *Jesus: A Life*, p. xi.
41. Wilson, *Jesus: A Life*, p. 201.

Chapter 6: Golgotha

42. Porter, *Jesus Christ: The Jesus of History, the Christ of Faith*, p. 117.
43. Boers, *Who Was Jesus?*, p. 91.
44. Wilson, *Jesus: A Life*, p. 210.
45. Crossan, *Jesus: A Revolutionary Biography*, p. 141.
46. Spoto, *Hidden Jesus*, p. 219.
47. Wilson, *Jesus: A Life*, p. xi.
48. Cross, *Who Was Jesus?*, p. 104.
49. Crossan, *Jesus: A Revolutionary Biography*, p. 197.

Epilogue: Aftermath

50. Edwin M. Yamauchi, "Easter: Myth,

Hallucination, or History?" Leadership U. www.leaderu.com/everystudent/easter/articles/yama.html.
51. Spoto, *Hidden Jesus*, p. 235.
52. Quoted in Yamauchi, "Easter: Myth, Hallucination, or History?"
53. Quoted in David Mishkin, "Did He or Didn't He? Jewish Views of the Resurrection of Jesus," Jews for Jesus. www.jewsforjesus.org/library/issues/11-06/didhe.htm.
54. Spoto, *The Hidden Jesus*, p. 237.
55. Quoted in The Preterist Archive, "Non-Occurrence of Prophecy Theories." *An Evening in Ephesus*. www.preteristarchive.com/StudyArchive/t/theory_nonocurence-prophecy.html.
56. Wilson, *Jesus: A Life*, p. 197.
57. Susan Perlman, "Y'shua—Let's Clear Things Up." Jews for Jesus. www.jewsforjesus.org/library/issues/09-05/yshualetsclear.htm.

For Further Reading

Books

Laurel Corona, *Religions of the World—Judaism*. San Diego, CA: Lucent Books, 2003. Traces the origins and development of the religion that not only survived frequent persecution, but also gave rise to two other major faiths—Islam and Christianity.

Richard Hanser, *Jesus: What Manner of Man Is This?* New York: Simon and Schuster, 1972. Traces the life and death of Jesus of Nazareth with special attention to his impact on world history.

William W. Lace, *Religions of the World—Christianity*. San Diego, CA: Lucent Books, 2005. Briefly describes the life of Jesus and then traces the development of Christianity from its humble beginning to one of the most powerful forces in history.

Stephen Mitchell, *Jesus: What He Really Said and Did*. New York: HarperCollins, 2002. A frank examination of some of the questions concerning the New Testament Gospels and how the teachings of Jesus can be seen in the light of those of other great religious leaders.

Neil Morris, *The Life of Jesus*. New York: Enchanted Lion Books, 2003. The life of Jesus is shown through some of the most famous paintings in the history of art. Particularly good at describing the symbolism behind some of the images.

Web Sites

Frontline: From Jesus to Christ (www.pbs.org/wgbh/pages/frontline/shows/religion). Interesting page adapted from Public Broadcasting System series with articles arranged by subject headings.

Ken Palmer *Life of Christ* (www.lifeofchrist.com). Well-organized site with information on the life, history, and teachings of Jesus.

Works Consulted

Books

Rudolf Augstein, *Jesus Son of Man*. Translated by Hugh Young. New York: Urizen Books, 1977. The author contrasts the beliefs and traditions of Christianity with what can be gleaned historically from the Gospels.

Hendrikus Boers, *Who Was Jesus?* New York: Harper and Row, 1989. The author examines the Gospels from a historical perspective in an attempt to explain Jesus's concept of his role and mission.

Rudolf Bultmann, *Jesus and the World*. Translated by Louise Pettibone Smith and Erminie Huntress Lantero. New York: Charles Scribner's Sons, 1934. Classic portrayal of Jesus in the context of his existence as a Jew in first-century Palestine.

Colin Cross, *Who Was Jesus?* New York: Atheneum, 1970. The author succeeds in giving a factual account of Jesus's life free of any religious bias.

John Dominic Crossan, *Jesus: A Revolutionary Biography*. New York: HarperCollins, 1989. The author seeks to identify historical truths about Jesus in order to explain who he was and what he taught.

Stevan L. Davies, *Jesus the Healer*. New York: Continuum, 1995. Jesus's healings and exorcisms examined from the standpoints of both first-century beliefs and modern medical knowledge.

John Drane, *Son of Man: A New Life of Christ*. Grand Rapids, MI: William B. Eerdmans, 1993. A lively account of Jesus with an excellent selection of photographs and sidebars.

Tim LaHaye, *Jesus: Who Is He?* Sisters, OR: Multnomah Books, 1996. Examination of Jesus's life from an orthodox Christian standpoint by the coauthor of the popular *Left Behind* series.

Malcolm Muggeridge, *Jesus: The Man Who Lives*. New York: Harper and Row, 1975. Written by an atheist who converted to Christianity in his sixties, this is more a testament of faith than a biography, though beautifully and wittily written.

Pheme Perkins, *Jesus as Teacher*. Cambridge, England: Cambridge University Press, 1990. A theologian's views and comments, not only on Jesus's message, but also on his style of teaching.

J.R. Porter, *Jesus Christ: The Jesus of History, the Christ of Faith*. New York: Oxford University Press, 1999. Large, lavishly illustrated volume that breaks Jesus's life and teachings into short, easily read segments.

Donald Spoto, *The Hidden Jesus*. New York: St. Martin's Press, 1998. Highly absorbing account of Jesus that combines the Gospel narratives with literary criticism, historical research, and theological scholarship.

A.N. Wilson, *Jesus: A Life*. New York: W.W. Norton, 1992. A hard, realistic look at the historically verifiable facts about Jesus as compared with what the author says are myths that grew up to surround his memory.

Internet Sources

The Arabic Gospel of the Infancy of the Savior, Chapter 38. Gnostic Society Library. www.gnosis.org/library/infarab.htm.

BELIEVE Religious Information Source. www.mb-soft.com/believe/txo.miracle.htm.

Susan S. Carroll, "The Star of Bethlehem: An Astronomical and Historical Perspective." Sciastro: An IRC Chat Channel Devoted To Amateur Astronomy. www.sciastro.net/portia/articles/thestar.htm.

Catholic Exchange. www.catholicexchange.com.

Pierre Gilbert, "Moving Toward Greatness." Canadian Mennonite University. www.cmu.ca/faculty/pgilbert/radio_messages/moving_toward_greatness.shtml.

Good News. www.goodnewsinc.net.

The Gospel of Mary Magdalene. The Gnostic Library Society. www.gnosis.org/library/marygosp.htm.

The Gospel of Peter. Early Christian Writings. www.earlychristianwritings.com/text.

H. Tracy Hall, "A Scientist Looks at the Miracles of Jesus." 50th Anniversary of Diamond Synthesis. www.htracyhall.org/pdf/miracles.pdf.

Greg Herrick, "Understanding the Meaning of the Term 'Disciple.'" Bible.org. www.bible.org/default.asp.

Jerusalem Perspective Online. www.jerusalemperspectiveonline.com.

Flavius Josephus, *Antiquities of the Jews*. Translated by William Whiston. *The Works of Flavius Josephus*. www.ccel.org/j/josephus/JOSEPHUS.HTM.

Anthony M. Ludovici, *Man: An Indictment*. www.anthonymludovici.com/mi_11.htm.

David Mishkin, "Did He or Didn't He? Jewish Views of the Resurrection of Jesus." Jews for Jesus. www.jewsforjesus.org/library/issues/11-06/didhe.htm.

New Advent, *The Gospel of Pseudo-Matthew*, Chapter 26. *The Fathers of the Church*. www.newadvent.org/fathers/0848.htm.

Susan Perlman, "Y'shua—Let's Clear Things Up." Jews for Jesus. http://jewsforjesus.org/library/issues/09-05/yshualetsclear.htm.

The Preterist Archive, "Non-Occurrence of Prophecy Theories." *An Evening in Ephesus*. www.preteristarchive.com/StudyArchive/t/theory_nonoccurence-prophecy.html.

The Protoevangelium of James. Roberts-Donaldson English Tranlation. Early Christian Writings. www.earlychristianwritings.com/text/infancyjamesroberts.html.

Religion-online.org. www.religiononline.org.

Barry D. Smith, *Life of Jesus*. Atlantic Baptist University, www.abu.nb.ca/Courses/NT Intro/LifeJ/IndexLife.htm.

James D. Tabor, "The Signs of the Messiah: 4Q521." *The Jewish Roman World of Jesus* (University of North Carolina - Charlotte Religious Studies Catalog). www.religiousstudies.uncc.edu/jdtabor/4q521.html.

Who Is Jesus? www.greatcom.org.

Ralph Wilson, "Judas' Betrayal." Jesus Walk Bible Study Series. www.jesuswalk.com/lessons/21_37-22_6.htm.

Edwin M. Yamauchi, "Easter: Myth, Hallucination, or History." Leadership U. www.leaderu.com/everystudent/easter/articles/yama.html.

Index

Abraham, 16, 18
Adam, 16, 33, 48
Alexander the Great, 16
Andrew, 50
angels, 19–20, 24
  John the Baptist's birth and, 42
  messages to Joseph and, 26–27, 32
Anna (mother of Mary), 18
Annas, 83
Anthony, Mark (Roman em-peror), 15
Antipater (Arab ruler), 15
Antiquities of the Jews (Josephus), 33
anti-Semitism, 87
apocryphal stories, 10–11
  Jesus's childhood and, 33–35
  see also Gnostic Gospels
Apostles, 42, 50–51
Arabic Infancy Gospel, 30–31, 35–36, 39
archaeology, 28, 32, 89
  Dead Sea Scrolls and, 43–44
Archelaus, (King of Judea) 32
Aristotle, 97
Asita, 30
astrology, 24–25

Augstein, Rudolf, 69

Babylonians, 74
Barabbas, 85–87
Bartholomew, 51
Beelzebub (Satan), 61
Bethlehem, 21
  description of, 22
  Gnostic version and, 23–25
  Jesus's birth and, 13–15, 22–23, 27
  magi and, 25–27
  Roman census and, 22–23
  slaughter of children in, 15, 25–26
  star of, 24, 97
Bhagavad Gita (Hindu writings), 30
Bible
  apocryphal additions to, 10–11
  Dead Sea Scrolls and, 43–44
  Gnostics and, 18
  Jesus's knowledge of, 37–40
  Mary's background and, 16
  prophecy and, 26, 70, 72
  see also specific books
Boers, Hendrikus, 13, 47, 72, 81

Bultmann, Rudolf, 58

Caesar, Augustus (Roman emperor), 15–16, 22
Caesar, Julius (Roman dictator), 15
Caiaphas, 73
  Jesus's interrogation by, 81–84
Calvary, 89
Carroll, Susan S., 24
Christianity, 87, 97
  Constantine's influence on, 10–11
  eternal life and, 55, 66
  faith and, 58–61, 64–65
  forgiveness and, 44, 46, 54–55
  John the Baptist and, 40
  Last Supper and, 77–78
  love and, 55, 62–66
  paradise and, 55
  popularity of, 8
  pride and, 56–57
  resurrection and, 61–62, 72, 93–97
  salvation and, 54–57, 70–71
  Sermon on the Mount and, 55–56
Church of Jesus Christ of Latter-day Saints, 42

Citlatonac (Aztec god), 20
Constantine (emperor of Rome), 10–11
Copernicus, 97
Corinth, 13
Corinthians, second letter to, 13
cross, 8, 92
Cross, Colin, 36, 45
Crossan, John Dominic, 14, 26, 51, 54, 75
crucifixion, 86–92
cures, 30–31, 33, 35, 57, 59–61
Cynics, 30

daggerman, 76
Damascus, 28
Daniel, book of, 66–67
David (king of Judea), 16, 18, 22–24
Dead Sea, 28
Dead Sea Scrolls, 43–44, 50
December 25 tradition, 27
discourse, 54
Drane, John, 45, 64, 67

Easter, 93
Eden, Garden of, 33, 48
Edom, 15
Egypt, 11
   flight to, 26–27
   pharaoh gods of, 13
   return from, 29–32
   slaughter of male children and, 26
   elementary school (*ben sefer*), 37
Elijah, 66
Elisha, 66
Elizabeth (Mary's cousin), 20–21
Essenes, 43–45, 65
eternal life, 55, 66
Eucharist ceremony, 78
Euclid, 97
Eve, 33, 48
Exodus, book of, 48
exorcism, 61–62

faith, 58–61, 64–65
forgiveness, 44, 46, 54–55

Gabriel, 20
Galilee, 21, 28, 32
   Herod Antipas and, 85
   Jesus's ministry and, 53–69
   religious climate of, 29
   reputation of, 29
   revolts in, 29
   Sea of, 28–29
Genesis, book of, 16
Gethsemane, Garden of, 78–81
Gilbert, Pierre, 59
Gnostic Gospels, 10–11
   Egyptian sojourn and, 30–32
   as fairy tales, 31–32
   forgiveness and, 44
   traditions of Mary and, 18–20, 23–25
God
   as father of Jesus, 19, 67, 69
   Holy Spirit and, 42–43
   Isaac's birth and, 18
   Kingdom of, 55–56, 58, 70, 77–78, 96
   Law and, 64
   love and, 55, 62–66
   miracles and, 45, 59
Golgotha, 89–92
Gospel of Mary Magdalene, 95
Gospels, 8–12
   genealogies in, 16
   Jesus's baptism and, 45–47
   Jesus's birth and, 13–16
   See also specific books
Great Rift Valley, 28
Greco-Roman architecture, 16
Greek language, 10–11
Greeks
   Cynics and, 30
   Hellenic culture of, 16, 29
   miracles and, 59
Gregory I, (pope), 95

Ben Ha'galgal, Yohanan, 89
Hall, Tracy H., 58
healing, 57, 59–61, 80
heaven, 55
Hercules, 13
Herod Antipas (governor of Galilee), 50, 85
Herodias, 50

Herod the Great (king of Judea), 16
   death of, 26–27, 29, 32
   as Edomite, 15
   magi and, 25
   slaughters male children, 25–26
   Temple construction by, 74
hidden (*apokruphos*) books, 10–11
Hidden Jesus, The (Spoto), 22, 45, 48
Hinduism, 20, 30
Holy Spirit, 19–20, 39
   Dead Sea Scrolls and, 43
   as God's force, 42
   Jesus's baptism and, 46–47
   Trinity teaching and, 42
Horus (Egyptian god), 48

Immanuel ("God with us"), 19
Infancy Gospel of Thomas, 35
Isaac, 18
Isaiah, book of, 19, 52, 70
Israel Antiquities Authority, 89

Jacob, 51
James, 32–33, 50–51
James the Lesser, 51
Jehovah's Witnesses, 42
Jeremiah, book of, 74
Jerusalem, 43
   Jesus's entry into, 72–73
   Jesus's final week and, 70–80
   Passover in, 73
   see also Temple of Jerusalem
Jesus
   ancestry of, 16
   apocryphal childhood stories of, 33–36
   arrest of, 80–81
   baptism of, 39–40, 45–47
   birth of, 13–16, 19–20, 23–27
   as carpenter, 34–36, 39–40
   Cynics and, 30
   disciples of, 50–52
   education of, 36–39
   execution of, 8–9, 86–92
   final week of, 70–80
   flogging of, 87–88
   as greater Moses, 26, 48
   impact of, 8, 12, 97
   interrogation of, 81–84
   Law and, 62–66
   love and, 62–66
   as Messiah, 13–14, 47
   ministry of, 51–52
   miracles of, 45, 50, 57–62, 80
   non-Christian references to, 11–12
   resurrection of, 93–97
   salvation and, 54–57
   scholarship of, 36–40, 62–63
   Scriptural knowledge of, 37–40
   siblings of, 32–33, 35, 52
   as son of God, 67, 69
   as son of Man, 66–67, 76, 84
   teaching methods of, 53–55
   temptations of, 47–48
   tomb of, 92–94
   trial of, 84–88
   in wilderness, 47–48
   women and, 48, 68–69
Jesus: A Life (A.N. Wilson), 79
Jesus: A Revolutionary Biography (Crossan), 51
Jesus Christ: the Jesus of History, the Christ of Faith (Porter), 61
Jews, 16
   education and, 36–37
   Hellenic influence on, 16, 29
   Jesus's challenge to, 62–64
   women and, 18–19, 48
Jezreel Valley, 28
Joachim (father of Mary), 18
John, book of, 8, 10–11
   Jesus's baptism and, 46
   John the Baptist and, 43, 49–50
John, 50
John the Baptist, 20–21, 39
   arrest of, 48–50
   birth of, 40–43

death of, 50
  as forerunner of Jesus, 42–43
  Jesus's baptism by, 45–47
  in the wilderness, 43
Jordan River, 28, 40
  Jesus's baptism and, 45–47
Joseph (brother), 32
Joseph (husband of Mary), 16, 18, 21, 29
  angelic messages to, 26–27, 32
  as carpenter, 32
  children of, 33
  flees to Egypt, 26–27
  as foster father, 39
  loses Jesus, 38
  Roman census and, 22–23
Joseph of Arimathea, 91–92
Josephus, Flavius, 12, 28, 33, 50
Joshua, book of, 28
Judaism, 15, 16
  firstborn males and, 18
  Galilee and, 29
  Hellenic influence on, 16
  Messianic death and, 95
  Passover and, 37–38, 70, 73–74, 84–85, 87
  purification and, 27, 29
  synagogues and, 36–37
  see also Law, Jewish
Judas (brother), 32
Judas Iscariot, 50–51, 75–78, 80
judgment, 55, 76–77

Kerioth, 76
kingdom of God, 55–56, 58
  earthly hopes for, 70
  Jesus's resurrection and, 96
  Last Supper and, 77–78
Krishna (Hindu god), 20, 30

Last Supper, 77–78
Law, Jewish, 29, 39
  God and, 64
  Jesus's arrest and, 81–82, 84
  Jesus's teachings and, 62–66
  Sabbath and, 66
  Sadducees and, 73
Lawrence, T.E., 47
Lazarus, 61–62, 72, 78, 96
legal issues, 81–84
Levi, 36
Life of Jesus (Smith), 19
Lord's Prayer, 11
lot casting, 90
Luke, book of, 8, 9–11, 16
  Holy Spirit and, 42
  Jesus's birth and, 20, 27
  Jesus's childhood and, 37–38
  John the Baptist and, 40, 42
  Roman census and, 29

magi, 24
Mark, book of, 8, 10–11
  John the Baptist and, 43–44

  virgin birth and, 20
Martha, 61, 77
Marx, Karl, 97
Mary (sister of Lazarus), 61, 77
Mary (mother), 15, 29, 52, 67
  background of, 16–18
  betrothal of, 18–19
  flees to Egypt, 26–27
  Gnostic traditions of, 18–20, 23–25
  loses Jesus, 38
  other children of, 33
  Roman census and, 22–23
  virginity of, 18–20
  Zechariah and, 20–22
Mary Magdalene, 10, 93–95
materialism, 56
Matthew, book of, 8, 10–11, 32
  genealogy in, 16
  Jesus's birth and, 20, 27
  magi and, 25
Matthew, 50–51
measuring stick (*kanon*), 11
Mediterranean Sea, 28
Messiah, 13–14, 47, 73
  Dead Sea Scrolls and, 43
  Jesus admits to being, 68–69
  Jewish expectations of, 16, 67, 77
  modern rabbis and, 95
  Romans and, 69
  as warrior, 50, 53, 55

Micah, book of, 22
miracles, 45, 50, 58
  casting out demons, 61–62
  healing, 57, 59–61, 80
  resurrections, 20, 61–62, 72, 93–97
  walking on water, 59
Miryam. *See* Mary
money changers, 74–75
Mormons, 42
Moses, 26, 48
Moule, C.F.D., 94
Muggeridge, Malcolm, 16, 47

Nativity accounts, 16, 23, 40, 43
Nazareth, 21, 27
  archaeological evidence and, 28, 32
  employment in, 32
  insignificance of, 28
  Joseph and, 32
  life in, 32–33
  rejects Jesus, 52
  Roman census and, 22–23
  synagogue of, 36–37
New Testament. *See* Bible
Nicodemus, 92
Noah's flood, 48
Numbers, book of, 25

Old Testament. *See* Bible
Olives, Mount of, 78–80

Palestine, 27
  culture of, 15–16
  Galilee and, 29
  political environment of, 15
  Roman census and, 22–23
parables, 54–56
paradise, 55
Passover, 37–38, 70, 73–74, 84–85, 87
Paul, 13, 20, 32, 47, 52
Perkins, Pheme, 51
Perlman, Susan, 97
persecution, 56
Persians, 89
Peter, 10, 69
  denies Jesus, 80, 83
  personality of, 59–60
  as Simon, 50
pharaoh, 26
Pharisees, 45
  influence of, 64
  Jesus's challenge to, 62–66, 73
  Law and, 62–65
  plot Jesus's death, 73
  resurrection and, 95–96
Philip, 51
Pilate, Pontius (Roman governor), 12, 27, 83, 92
  Jesus' trial and, 84–88
Plato, 97
Pompey, 15
Porter, J.R., 20, 47, 61–62, 64, 67
pride, 56–57
prophecy, 26, 70, 72
prostitutes, 66
proto-Mark, 11
Pseudo-Matthew, 35–36
purification, 27, 29, 44

"Q" *(quelle)* source, 11–12
Quesalcote (Aztec god), 20
Quirinius (governor of Syria), 22, 27
Qumran community, 43–44

rabbis, 53, 95
Regulus (star), 24
resurrection, 61–62, 72
  critics of, 96–97
  global impact of, 97
  of Jesus, 93–97
  Pharisees and, 95–96
Roman Catholic Church, 95
Romans
  census by, 22–23, 29
  destroy Temple, 75
  Galilee and, 29
  Jesus's punishment by, 87–92
  Jewish Messiah and, 69
  Jewish priests and, 83
  law of, 81–82
  Palestinian politics and, 15

Sabbath, 66, 92
Sadducees, 63–65, 73
Safrai, Shmuel, 37
Salome, 50
salvation, 54–55
  barriers to, 56–57
  Jesus's death by, 70–71
Samaritans, 68–69

Sanhedrin (Jewish court), 73, 92
   Jesus's interrogation by, 81–84
Sarah, 18
Satan, 47–48, 61, 76
"Scientist Looks at the Miracles of Jesus, A" (Hall), 58
Scopus, Mount, 89
secondary school (*bet midrash*), 37
second coming, 96–97
Sepphoris, 32, 82
Sermon on the Mount, 53, 55–56
Set (Egyptian god), 48
Shroud of Turin, 91
Sidon, 61
Simeon, 30–31
Simon (brother), 32
Simon of Cyrene, 89
Simon the Zealot, 50–51
sin, 48, 63, 66
Sinai, Mount, 47–48
Slaughter of the Innocents, 15, 25–26
Smith, Barry, 19, 46, 61
Solomon (king of Judea), 74
son of Man, 66–67, 76, 84
Son of Man (Drane), 45, 67
Spiceland, J.D., 59

Spoto, Donald, 22, 45, 48, 55, 87, 93, 96
"Star of Bethlehem: An Astro-nomical and Historical Per-spective, The" (Carroll), 24
Stolper, Pinchus, 96–97
suffocation, 89–90
swords, 78–79
synagogues, 36–37

tax collectors, 50, 66
Temple of Jerusalem, 15, 18, 27
   Jesus's teachings and, 53
   money changers in, 74–75
   purification and, 29
   Roman destruction of, 75
   Scriptural knowledge and, 37
   Simeon and, 30–31
Tertullian, 42
Thaddeus, 51
Thomas, 10, 51
tomb guards, 95
Torah, 37
Trinity teaching, 42
Tyre, 61
Tzaferis, Vassilios, 89
Unitarians, 42

Venus, 24

Via Dolorosa ("Way of Suffering"), 88–89
Via Maris route, 28
virgin birth, 18–20, 27
   Gnostic version of, 23–25
   Jesus's siblings and, 32–33
   magi and, 25–27
   purification and, 27, 29
   slaughter of male children after, 15, 25–26

Web sites, 24, 33, 58, 76, 95, 101
Who Was Jesus? (Cross), 36
Wilson, A.N., 75, 78–80, 83, 87, 97
Wilson, Ralph, 76
women, 18, 48, 68
Works of Flavius Josephus, The, 33

Yeshus. *See* Jesus
Yu (emperor of China), 13
Yusuf. *See* Joseph (husband of Mary)

Zachyas, 35–36
Zealots, 29, 50, 76
Zechariah, book of, 72, 76
Zechariah (father of John the Baptist), 20–22, 42
Zoraster, 20

Picture Credits

Cover photo: © Elio Ciol/CORBIS
© Alinari Archives/CORBIS, 41, 77
© Archivo Iconografico S.A./CORBIS, 7 (upper left), 21, 31, 46, 82, 90, 96
© Arte & Immagini srl/CORBIS, 51, 71
© Brooklyn Museum of Art/CORBIS, 34
© Akexander Burkatovski/CORBIS, 65
© Burstein Collection/CORBIS, 26
Cameraphoto Arte, Venice/Art Resource, NY, 6 (lower right), 85
© Geoffrey Clements/CORBIS, 72
Corel Corporation, 6 (top), 7 (upper and lower right)
© Christie's Images/CORBIS, 25
© Elio Ciol/CORBIS, 9
Giraudon/Art Resource, NY, 74
©David Lees/CORBIS, 91
Erich Lessing/Art Resource, NY, 14, 15, 38, 49, 57, 63, 75, 79, 86, 94
Francis G. Mayer/CORBIS, 17
© Ali Meyer/CORBIS, 88
Photos.com, 6 (lower left), 19
Réunion des Musées Nationaux/Art Resource, NY, 7 (lower left), 56, 60, 68
Scala/Art Resource, NY, 44, 54
© Stapleton Collection/CORBIS, 10
Time Life Pictures/Getty Images, 29
Steve Zmina, 23

About the Author

William W. Lace is a native of Fort Worth, Texas, where he is executive assistant to the chancellor at Tarrant County College. He holds a bachelor's degree from Texas Christian University, a master's degree from East Texas State, and a doctorate from the University of North Texas. Prior to joining Tarrant County College, he was director of the News Service at the University of Texas at Arlington and a writer and columnist for the *Fort Worth Star-Telegram*. He has written more than twenty-five books for Lucent, one of which—*The Death Camps*—was selected by the New York Public Library for its 1999 Recommended Teenage Reading List. He and his wife, Laura, a retired school librarian, live in Arlington, Texas, and have two children and three grandchildren.

DISCARD